The Workplace

INTERPERSONAL STRENGTHS AND LEADERSHIP

Dr. Joe Pace

Mc
Graw
Hill

Boston   Burr Ridge, IL   Dubuque, IA   Madison, WI   New York   San Francisco   St. Louis
Bangkok   Bogotá   Caracas   Kuala Lumpur   Lisbon   London   Madrid   Mexico City
Milan   Montreal   New Delhi   Santiago   Seoul   Singapore   Sydney   Taipei   Toronto

The McGraw-Hill Companies

Higher Education

McGraw-Hill Higher Education
A Division of The McGraw-Hill Companies

THE PROFESSIONAL DEVELOPMENT SERIES: BOOK TWO: THE WORKPLACE: INTERPERSONAL STRENGTHS AND LEADERSHIP
Published by McGraw-Hill, a business unit of The McGraw-Hill Companies, Inc., 1221 Avenue of the Americas, New York, NY, 10020.
Copyright © 2006 by The McGraw-Hill Companies, Inc. All rights reserved. No part of this publication may be reproduced or distributed in any form or by any means, or stored in a database or retrieval system, without the prior written consent of The McGraw-Hill Companies, Inc., including, but not limited to, in any network or other electronic storage or transmission, or broadcast for distance learning.
Some ancillaries, including electronic and print components, may not be available to customers outside the United States.
This book is printed on acid-free paper.

9 0 ROV 15 14 13 12 11

ISBN   978-0-07-860569-7
MHID   0-07-860569-5

Publisher: *Emily Barrosse*
Executive editor: *David S. Patterson*
Developmental editor: *Anne Sachs*
Senior marketing manager: *Leslie Oberhuber*
Senior media producer: *Todd Vaccaro*
Project manager: *Jean R. Starr*
Production supervisor: *Janean A. Utley*
Associate designer: *Srdjan Savanovic*
Media project manager: *Nadia Bidwell*
Photo research coordinator: *Natalia C. Peschiera*
Art editor: *Ayelet Arbel*
Art director: *Jeanne Schreiber*
Cover photo: © *Jack Hollingsworth/Getty Images*
Typeface: *9.5/12 Palatino*
Compositor: *Carlisle Communications, Ltd.*
Printer: *Von Hoffmann/Custom*

www.mhhe.com

Contents

As a psychologist and former college president involved in higher education for over thirty-six years, I often have been asked what skills most directly contribute to career success.

The questioner generally expects me to talk about job skills. Thirty years ago, it would have been typing. Today, it might be familiarity with common workplace software.

But the fact is that most employers don't care how fast you type or how well you align columns on a spreadsheet.

What Do Employers Want?

In a recent survey,* business owners and corporate executives in the United States were asked to rate what they valued most in a new employee:

- Dependability—35%
- Honesty—27%
- Good attitude—19%
- Competence—19%*

What does this tell us? It says, simply, that 81 percent of corporations in the United States rate the personal qualities of dependability, honesty, and attitude—what I call *professionalism*—above any skills-based competencies.

The Need for *Professionalism*

Does it make sense that employers value professionalism over what we generally think of as job-related skills? Certainly. All jobs and businesses are different. Even companies manufacturing similar products in the same city will have their own unique procedures and policies. Working for one does not mean you can easily transition into working for another. Employers know this. They know that they will have to train you in the skills necessary for your job, and they are willing to do this. What employers want from you are the internal qualities that make you trainable.

Employers want you to be reliable; they want you to be hardworking; and they want you to be ethical. In a word, employers look for the qualities that make a person *professional*.

*Padgett Business Services, quarterly survey of service and retail clients.

Why *The Professional Development Series?*

The sad fact is that most colleges and schools spend an overwhelming majority of the time and energy developing hard skills while ignoring the personal qualities of character and dependability that actually get people hired. The good news is that—like typing or programming—professionalism can be taught.

My aim in developing this *Professional Development Series* has been to teach the personal skills that lead to job and career success. The *Series* is based on both my own research on career success and my experience as a lecturer, college president, and mentor. The material I present in the *Series* is the same material I have used to guide thousands of students and to train hundreds of instructors across North America. The goal for teachers who use the *Series* is to help turn out graduates ready to meet the challenges of the fast-paced professional world. The goal for students learning with the *Series* is to succeed in their chosen careers and, more importantly, to succeed in life.

The Books in *The Professional Development Series*

The *Professional Development Series* is easy to read and user-friendly. The books are brief, because you are busy. The books are practical, because you need specific guidance, not vague assurances. Each book and every chapter use a consistent organization of text and features to structure the material.

Book 1: The Workplace: Today and Tomorrow

Book One is an orientation to the world of work. In it, you will consider the occupations that are most likely to have job openings in the coming years, how to prepare yourself to fill these openings, and what the workplace environment is like in the twenty-first century. Professional business protocol, professional presence, and a customer-first attitude also are explored and discussed.

Book 2: The Workplace: Interpersonal Strengths and Leadership

Professional success in the twenty-first century demands that people work together to achieve their goals. Book 2: *Interpersonal Strengths and Leadership* explores and develops the skills that make a person a good teammate and a good leader. Developing a standard of excellence and pride in your work along with understanding ethics, trust, and respect also is covered. Thinking strategically and modeling leadership techniques are addressed as well.

Book 3: The Workplace: Personal Skills for Success

Time management and stress management come to mind when we talk about *Personal Skills for Success*. In Book I, you will develop and practice these skills. You also will be encouraged to think about who you are and what you believe and to use what you learn to establish goals for the future and to develop a plan to achieve those goals. Communicating and presenting ideas and concepts, as well as thinking critically and creatively, also are covered.

Book 4: The Workplace: Chart Your Career

One day you leave school and you have a job; twenty years later you look back and realize that you have a career. How can you make sure that the career you have is fulfilling and rewarding? How can you avoid or overcome the inevitable missteps—taking the wrong job, for example—and get your career back on track? Book 4 offers guidance on planning a career and, more importantly, on developing, changing, and maintaining it.

Features of Each Book in *The Professional Development Series*

Every chapter of each book has a consistent format, clearly organizing the material to help you learn.

Beginning Each Chapter

What Will You Do? The entire plan for the chapter is set out in What Will You Do? Each section within the chapter is called out with a one-sentence summary describing the content.

Why Do You Need to Know This? The information in each chapter is there for a reason. Why Do You Need to Know This? explains how the material will be useful in finding a job, building a rewarding career, or succeeding in life.

Set the Pace Before beginning a chapter, it is important to determine what you already know about the topic. Set the Pace asks you to think about your own experiences with the subject.

Objectives These are your goals for the chapter. When you have done the reading and the work for each chapter, you should have learned about and practiced each of the bulleted skills. These Objectives will be revisited in the Chapter Summary.

Beginning Each Section

Reading and Study Tip Each tip presents a helpful suggestion to aid your retention of the material in the section.

In Each Section

Quotations These thoughts offer inspiration, context, and perspective from important and influential people in all walks of life.

Vocabulary Important terms are called out in the margins and defined.

New Attitudes/New Opportunities These profiles present real people giving voice to their real-world goals, concerns, and experiences.

Pace Points Techniques and advice that I have found useful from my own work experience.

Judgment Call These real-world scenarios call on you to interpret and act on the information in the section. Check your answers online at *www.mhhe.com/pace*.

Dr. Joe Pace These are quotations from my workshops that, over time, my students have found the most meaningful.

Ending Each Section

Quick Recap Here is a summary to help you review the section material, check yourself with short review questions, and check your answers online at *www.mhhe.com/pace*.

Chapter Review and Activities

Chapter Summary The chapter's Objectives reappear here with a review of what you should know about each section and about each objective.

Business Vocabulary All the vocabulary terms from the chapter are listed with the page number where they can be found within the chapter. Double-check to make sure you know what each word means and how it is used.

Key Concept Review Short-answer questions in the Key Concept Review will help you remember the material from each section.

Online Project Go online to learn more about what you have learned in the chapter.

Step Up the Pace These real-world scenarios help you think about applying what you have learned in the chapter to your own life, job, and career.

Business Skills Brush-Up This activity gives you the chance to practice important business skills such as critical reading and effective writing.

Support for *The Professional Development Series*

The books of the *Series* are supported by *Professional Development Series* **website (www.mhhe.com/pace)** On the website, students can find answers to questions posed in the text, additional chapter review materials, and topics for additional reading and study. Instructors also can access sample syllabi, suggested test questions, and tips for teaching.

Study Smart **Study Skills Tutorial** From time management to taking notes, *Study Smart* is an excellent way to practice your skills. *Study Smart* was developed by Andrea Bonner and Mieke Schipper of Sir Sanford Fleming College and is available on CD-ROM (0–07–245515–2). This innovative study skills tutorial teaches students essential note-taking methods, test-taking strategies, and time management secrets. *Study Smart* is free when packaged with the books of *The Professional Development Series*.

BusinessWeek **Online** Interested instructors can offer their students 15 weeks of access to *BusinessWeek* Online by requesting that a password card be packaged with the books of *The Professional Development Series*. For further information call 1–800–338–3987 or speak to your McGraw-Hill Sales Representative.

Instructor's Resource **CD-ROM** This is a thorough guide to planning, organizing, and administering courses using *The Professional Development Series*. The CD includes sample syllabi, model assessments, and test questions, and teaching tips for each section in every chapter of all four books.

About the Author

For over thirty-six years, Dr. Joe Pace has been a nationally recognized speaker, author, and educator. A psychologist and former college president, Dr. Pace currently serves as the managing partner of the Education Initiative for The Pacific Institute.

Dr. Pace is creator of the *Success Strategies for Effective Colleges and Schools* program implemented worldwide in over 200 colleges and schools. He has served as commissioner of the Accrediting Council of Independent Colleges and Schools (ACICS) in Washington, D.C.; on the board of directors of The Association of Independent Colleges and Schools, now known as the CCA (Career College Association); and as president of the Florida Association of Postsecondary Schools and Colleges.

A popular keynote speaker at conferences and conventions, Dr. Pace also has conducted a variety of seminars and workshops throughout North America on such topics as school management, faculty development, student retention, psychology, and motivation. Thousands of college-level students have benefited from his expertise in the areas of psychology, personal development, and business administration.

Dr. Pace is known for his warmth, enthusiasm, humor, and "intelligent heart." His audiences enjoy his genuine spirit and heartwarming stories. Because of his loving and caring nature, Dr. Pace is able to help people to succeed in their chosen careers, but more importantly, to succeed in life.

Acknowledgments

The energy to develop this series has come from my family: my wife Sharon, my daughters Tami and Tiffany, my son-in-law John, and my grandkids Nicholas, Jessica, Dylan, and Jonathan. Their love and support get me up in the morning, inspire my work, and excite me about tomorrow.

Thanks also to Shawn Knieriem, my director of operations, for her assistance and support with this project.

My special thanks to the Advisory Board and Review Panel for their excellent suggestions, tips, techniques, and wisdom, as well as for their time and effort in attending various meetings. I have considered them friends and colleagues for many years, and it was an honor to work with them on this project.

Advisory Board In October of 2002, a group of educators came together to chart the course for the project that would become *The Professional Development Series.* Their insights and vision guided me.

Teresa Beatty, ECPI

Gary Carlson, ITT Educational Services

Jerry Gallentine, National American University

Gery Hochanadel, Keiser College

Jim Howard, Sanford Brown Colleges

Ken Konesco, Indiana Business Colleges

Review Panel Once the Board provided the goal, the Review Panel undertook to develop the project. Their sage advice influenced every page of *The Professional Development Series.*

Steve Calabro, Southwest Florida College

JoAnna Downey, Corinthian Colleges

Barb Gillespie, Cuyamaca College

Lynn Judy, Carteret Community College

Ken Konesco, Indiana Business Colleges

Ada Malcioln, International Institute of the Americas

Dena Montiel, Santa Ana School of Continuing Education

Peggy Patlan, Fox College

Sharon Roseman, Computer Career Center

Peggy Schlechter, National American University

The Workplace

Develop a Standard of Excellence

What Will You Do?

1.1 Be Well Informed Examine the types of knowledge you need to be well informed, have confidence to make decisions, develop ideas, and do excellent work.

1.2 Be Responsible, Take Initiative, Make Decisions Learn what it means to be responsible, take initiative, and make excellent decisions.

1.3 Be Precise Learn how to be precise and go the extra mile to ensure high-quality, excellent work.

1.4 Develop Personal and Professional Ethics Examine the role of personal and professional ethics and how they affect decisions and contribute to your standard of excellence.

1.5 Take Pride in Your Work Learn to enjoy what you do, be proud of your work, and apply your standard of excellence to everything that you do.

Why Do You Need to Know This?

In the workplace, your work is a direct reflection of your value as an employee. Caring about what you do and how you do it will help you become a successful professional. Maintaining a high standard of excellence will ensure that everything you do, from filing papers to giving a presentation, is excellent. When you do excellent work, you are an asset to your company. When you go home at the end of each day, you can be proud of what you have achieved. If you take yourself and your work seriously, your colleagues will do the same. This chapter will teach you how you can develop a standard of excellence, so you will do excellent work and be respected as a true professional.

Chapter Objectives

After completing this chapter, you will be able to:

- Define and acquire the knowledge you need to be well informed and do excellent work.

- Be responsible, take initiative, and make excellent decisions.

- Be precise and accurate and go the extra mile to ensure excellence in everything you do.

- Identify your personal and professional ethics and learn how to deal with misconduct and harassment.

- Take pride in your work by maintaining your standard of excellence.

Set the *Pace*

A Standard of Excellence   You expect a certain level of quality when you buy a product or eat at a restaurant. If what you receive is less than excellent, you would probably not be satisfied. Think about some of the standards of quality you have as a customer.

- What kind of service do you expect?
- What makes a meal or a product excellent?
- What do you consider below your standards?

Activity   Write two or three paragraphs explaining the standards you have for the things you buy and how those standards can be applied to the things you do. Share your thoughts with your classmates during a discussion about the importance of setting standards.

Be Well Informed

Have you ever been in a conversation where you felt you didn't have anything to contribute? Have you ever sweated over a question because you didn't know the answer? You are probably reading this chapter about being well informed now so that you can avoid that insecure feeling in class. When you discuss this chapter in class, you won't worry if your instructor asks you why being well informed is important. You will raise your hand confidently and answer correctly because you will know the answer. When you are well informed, you possess the knowledge and information you need to answer questions, give opinions, make decisions, and develop new ideas. You know what to do, how to do it, and how to do it well. When you are well informed, you have the confidence to act, and act wisely.

The Encyclopedia of the Mind   The knowledge you possess is stored like a reference book in your head—an encyclopedia of the mind. Your mind contains all the information you have learned in the course of your life. This includes everything from knowing that if you touch something hot you will get burned, to knowing that $7 \times 7 = 49$, to knowing how to handle your grumpy boss. This section will tell you how you can fill that encyclopedia with the kinds of knowledge you need to be well informed and do excellent work.

Reading and Study Tip

Examples
Look for paragraphs that illustrate ideas with examples. Think of two examples of your own for an important idea presented in this section. Write them down on a separate sheet of paper.

Types of Knowledge

To be well informed, you have to possess knowledge. Our knowledge is of two types: personal and practical. Knowledge can be

- Things you learned as a child (hot stoves can burn skin).
- Things you learned in school (the square root of 49 is 7).
- Things you've learned on your own (don't bother your boss until after his or her morning coffee).

What You Know

Personal knowledge is information that we know or believe, without having to actually think about it. We learn most of our personal knowledge from experience:

- By being shown by our families or mentors.
- Through trial and error.

> *Knowledge is of two kinds. We know a subject ourselves, or we know where we can look up information on it.*
>
> *Samuel Johnson*
> *18th-Century British Writer*

Personal knowledge is unique to every person. Our personal knowledge becomes automatic because we use it so much. How to drive a car is a good example of personal knowledge. Once you have enough experience, driving becomes automatic and hard to explain without actually doing it. Personal knowledge colors how we think and understand, and determines our individual point of view.

What You Learn

Practical knowledge is structured information or skills we memorize or practice. We learn most of our practical knowledge from

- A classroom.
- Books and media.
- Formal training and study.

Practical knowledge can be written using numbers or words and explained to everyone in the same way. The multiplication tables or facts and dates are examples of practical knowledge.

Knowledge You Need to Succeed

Another way to think of personal knowledge and practical knowledge is to think of them as street smarts and book smarts. These phrases describe a person's knowledge strength. Knowledge strength is the area or type of knowledge that you are strongest in. Here's an example of two people with different kinds of "smarts":

<table>
<tr>
<td>

Teresa's knowledge strength is her street smarts; she

- Is very clever.
- Is good at dealing with people.
- Trusts her instincts and beliefs.
- Can think on her feet.
- Always gets in and out of situations with no problems.

Teresa relies heavily on her personal knowledge, her instincts, and her experiences to succeed.

</td>
<td>

Matt's knowledge strength is his book smarts; he is

- Very intelligent.
- Good at explaining ideas and concepts.
- Full of different facts and information.
- Good at understanding theories and formulas.
- Good at following instructions and making rules.

Matt uses the practical knowledge that he has been taught in school or from books to get through life.

</td>
</tr>
</table>

Street Smarts, Book Smarts, or Both?

Knowledge is a tool that you rely on to help you handle different situations successfully. When you have only one type of knowledge that is suited to one type of situation, your ability to make good decisions is limited. To be well informed, you need to have both kinds of knowledge.

Scenario: Matt and Teresa are going to buy a car together. They decide to go to "Honest Joe's" Used Car Lot.

- Matt does research on buying a car, the car they want and the cost, and the options for financing it.
- Teresa asks a mechanic what she should look for when buying a used car.
- Matt picks out a car they both like and agrees to pay the asking price.
- Teresa notices that Joe won't look her in the eye and takes a better look at the car.

Teresa finds some minor damage to the interior and offers Joe $500.00 less than the listed price. They make the deal and sit down to work out the financing. Joe offers them two payment options:

- No payment for three months and then an extra interest payment for every month after.

Figure 1.1 *Types of Knowledge*

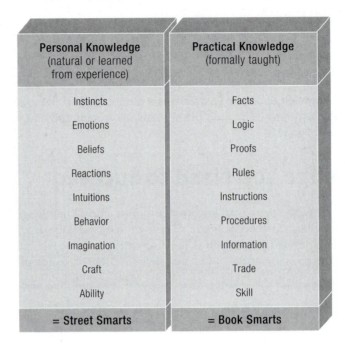

Personal Knowledge (natural or learned from experience)	Practical Knowledge (formally taught)
Instincts	Facts
Emotions	Logic
Beliefs	Proofs
Reactions	Rules
Intuitions	Instructions
Behavior	Procedures
Imagination	Information
Craft	Trade
Ability	Skill
= Street Smarts	**= Book Smarts**

Thinking Critically Think about all the kinds of information you know. *Are you more "street smart" or "book smart?"*

OR

• A higher monthly payment starting immediately but with a lower interest rate.

Teresa wants to take the car without having to put any money down. Matt refers to his research, calculates the numbers, and accepts the second deal, which works out to be less expensive.

Common Sense

When Matt and Teresa combined their knowledge strengths, they made a really good deal. On their own, both would have paid extra for the car. To be well informed, it's important to have both personal and practical knowledge strength. When you combine street smarts (personal knowledge) with book smarts (practical knowledge), you get common sense. You want to be able to apply common sense to everything you do. This means using your practical knowledge, like Matt, and your personal knowledge, like Teresa, to make the best decision.

Test Yourself

Here is a quick quiz to guide you in your thinking about what your knowledge strengths and weaknesses are.

1. You just bought a cell phone with new features that you have never used before. You want to figure out how to store a number in the phone book. Do you . . .
   a. Get out the instruction manual and read the directions for storing a number?
   b. Start scrolling through the menu and trying options until you figure it out?
   c. Read the basic directions and, once you are on the right track, figure the rest out on your own?

2. A customer calls your office complaining that a product he bought is faulty and asks for double his money back. Do you . . .
   a. Refuse to take the call until you have looked up your company's policy on returns?
   b. Listen to the person and get a feeling whether his complaint is genuine before dealing with the complaint?
   c. Tell the person you would be glad to help, if he or she would send you a copy of the receipt and a letter explaining the problem so you can process the complaint?

3. Your boss asks you to find sales figures from last year for a report. Do you . . .
   a. Go straight to the accounting archives and look up the company's annual report?
   b. Go straight to the accounting department and ask a friend there if she knows this information?
   c. Look up the annual report online, and then call the accounting department to confirm your numbers and ask for any other information you need?

We learn by doing and by studying.

How Did You Score? Read below to check what your knowledge strength is.

- If you answered (a) for at least two questions, then you rely heavily on your practical knowledge strength and need to develop your personal knowledge strength.
- If you answered (b) for at least two questions, then you rely on your personal knowledge strength, so you should build your practical knowledge strength.
- If you answered (c) for at least two questions, congratulations! You use common sense in order to make decisions and answer questions.

Whatever your answers were, you should use what you do know and learn what you don't. Even if you found that you have a good balance of knowledge strength and use common sense, your work is not done yet. There is no limit to knowledge: As people, we have an infinite ability to learn. Even if you feel as if you know enough to do your job and get by, you can always do your job better by learning more.

Knowledge as an Asset

asset a valuable possession

An **asset** is a valuable possession. Knowledge is your biggest asset as an employee. The more you know by being well informed and using common sense, the more valuable you are to your company. *What* you know, however, is just as important as *how much* you know.

What You Should Know

If you ever watch trivia game shows on TV, you know that there are endless topics in which a person can gain expertise. In your work, you don't need knowledge in as many topics as a game show contestant, but in order to be well informed, you should have knowledge strength in three topics:

- General knowledge.
- Knowledge of your industry.
- Knowledge specific to the job that you do (*see* Figure 1.2).

Figure 1.2 *Essential Knowledge*

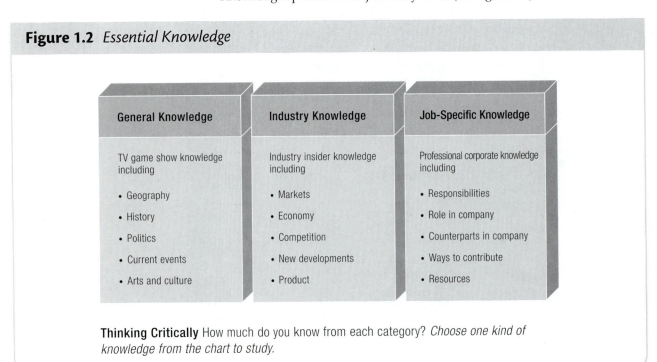

General Knowledge	Industry Knowledge	Job-Specific Knowledge
TV game show knowledge including	Industry insider knowledge including	Professional corporate knowledge including
• Geography	• Markets	• Responsibilities
• History	• Economy	• Role in company
• Politics	• Competition	• Counterparts in company
• Current events	• New developments	• Ways to contribute
• Arts and culture	• Product	• Resources

Thinking Critically How much do you know from each category? *Choose one kind of knowledge from the chart to study.*

Riddle Me This

You may wonder why you need to know about geography, for example, to do a job as a secretary. Here's a little riddle where knowledge of geography will help you solve the problem:

You work in Boston for an insurance company. Your boss is on a tour of the company's regional offices in Houston, Denver, and San Francisco. She tells you that she has 10:00 AM appointments at each office, on each day of her three-day trip. She asks you to give her a call at each office when she is there. Each day you call the office she is visiting at 10:00 sharp. Each day you ask for your boss and the receptionist tells you your boss isn't there yet. What are you doing wrong?

If you know your geography, you know that each city is in a different time zone from Boston. So when you call from Boston at 10:00, it is 9:00 AM in Houston, 7:00 AM in Denver, and 6:00 AM in San Francisco. You never know when general knowledge will come in handy. This is one reason why you should be as well informed as possible.

Knowledge = Ideas

The knowledge you bring to your work is an asset because it helps you come up with new ideas. See Figure 1.3 and read the following example.

Figure 1.3 *Using Knowledge*

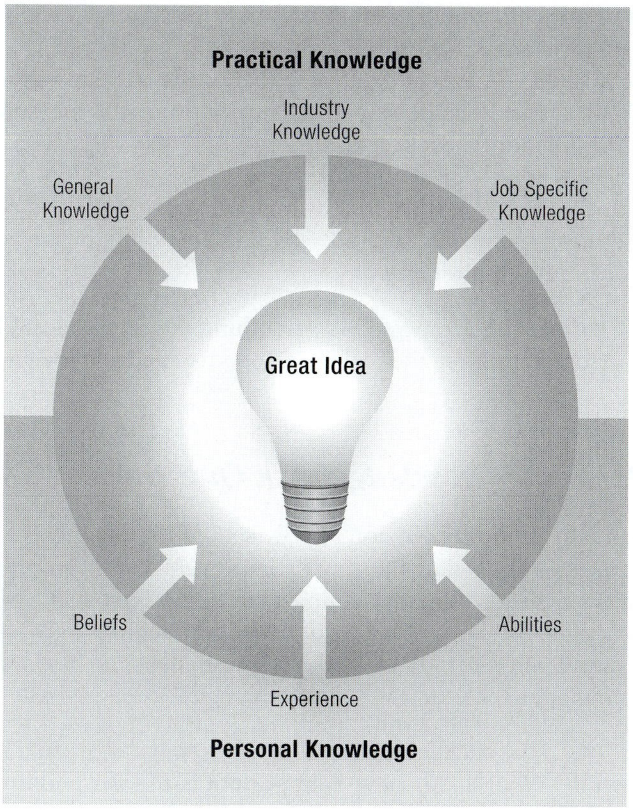

Thinking Critically Combine your street smarts and book smarts to make your ideas happen. *How does having knowledge strength in different topics help you come up with better ideas?*

You work for a new clothing company promoting their design label. You read in the Arts and Culture section of the paper that a famous recording artist from your area will be coming into town for a children's charity basketball game. You know from your personal knowledge that when a celebrity is seen wearing a clothing label, it helps sales. You decide that your company should donate T-shirts for the event. You realize this would be a great way to help the youth in your community and promote your company. You calculate the costs and realize that donating T-shirts will cost less than buying an advertisement in the paper. You also know that taking part in this event is great publicity because your company is helping a popular celebrity help your community.

How to Get the Information You Need

You can develop the practical and personal knowledge you need to be well informed by doing your homework and asking questions.

Develop Practical Knowledge: Do Your Homework

Doing your homework is the best way to build your practical knowledge strength. This means doing research, reading, studying specific topics, and even watching TV.

- **General Knowledge**
  The best way to build your general knowledge is to get in the habit of watching your local and national news. The news will keep you up-to-date on what's happening in your community and the world.
- **Industry Knowledge**
  Read the business section of the newspaper or the trade magazines lying around your office. Keep updated on the new products, companies, and competition in your field.
- **Job-Specific Knowledge**
  Read your company's history and its mission statement. Read company newsletters and memos to find out why you are doing the job you are and how it contributes to the company.

In each of these cases, if you come across something you don't know, head to your local library and look it up! Use the real encyclopedia to add to the encyclopedia of your mind.

Develop Personal Knowledge: Ask Questions

There is no shame in admitting we don't know something as long as we are willing to learn. The same goes for asking questions. Employers respect employees who ask questions because it means they are willing to listen and learn. An employee who asks questions avoids mistakes by asking how to do something right instead of staying uninformed and getting it wrong. Asking questions is the best way to develop the personal knowledge that you can't get from books or magazines.

- **Beliefs**
  Ask yourself, "What do I believe is important in my job, and important in my life?" "Do I believe my instincts, or should I find out more?" Ask questions about yourself and how you work so you will learn to trust your personal knowledge.

Pace Points

Questions?

There is no such thing as a stupid question. Most people will be glad to answer your questions, but they can't help you unless you ask.

- **Experience**
  Ask people with more experience for advice. You can ask your parents, mentors, colleagues, or boss.
- **Abilities**
  Ask your supervisors or colleagues for help. If you don't know how to run a computer program, ask someone in your tech department to show you.

Knowledge as Capital

Capital means wealth or resources. In today's business world, employers think of knowledge as capital. There is a whole movement in business called knowledge management, where employers capitalize on their employees' diverse knowledge. To **capitalize on** means to benefit from. Employers look for employees who are well informed and bring knowledge, creativity, and a fresh outlook to their work. Don't be content just knowing how to do your job; know how to do your job well. Capitalize on your knowledge of your job, your industry, and the world you live in to help you do excellent work.

capital wealth or resources in the form of money or property

capitalize on benefit from or use to your advantage

QUICK RECAP 1.1

BE WELL INFORMED

- When you are well informed, you can confidently answer questions, give opinions, make decisions, and come up with new ideas.
- In order to be well informed, you need to possess both practical and personal knowledge.
- You should have well-rounded knowledge strength to develop common sense.
- Knowledge is an asset that always comes in handy and leads to good ideas.
- Your knowledge capital helps you do excellent work and become an asset to your company.

CHECK YOURSELF

1. List the two types of knowledge discussed in this section.
2. Name one topic of general knowledge you should be informed about.

Check your answers online at **www.mhhe.com/pace**.

BUSINESS VOCABULARY

asset   a valuable possession
capital   wealth or resources in the form of money or property
capitalize on   benefit from or use to your advantage

Be Responsible, Take Initiative, Make Decisions

Why are you reading this book right now? You are probably reading this book because you made a decision to improve your career and you want to learn how. Congratulations, you are taking initiative. To **take initiative** means to take action without being asked or told to do so. When you take initiative, you make decisions for yourself and you make them happen. Employers are looking for employees who take initiative. True professionals don't wait to be told what to do—they notice a job that needs doing and do it.

In the Driver's Seat   Do you remember the first time you ever drove by yourself? It was probably a great feeling of freedom and independence, but it was also a little scary. That's because when you are in the driver's seat, you are in control, but you are also responsible. To be **responsible** means to consider the consequences of your actions when you make decisions. The goal of all professionals is to be in the driver's seat. You want to be in control of your career, do your own work, and make your own decisions. To get in the driver's seat, you have to demonstrate that you are responsible by taking initiative and making excellent decisions.

take initiative act of your own accord

responsible (1) to be reliable and trustworthy and concerned for your responsibilities; (2) to be accountable or answerable for actions, jobs, people, or things

reliable dependable

accountable responsible or answerable for a person, action, or thing

Being Responsible

The first step to getting into the driver's seat is to prove to your employers that you are responsible. You want your supervisors to trust your decisions and respect you as an equal. This respect has to be earned by being reliable and trustworthy. When you are **reliable,** you are dependable.

A responsible person always takes into consideration the consequences of his or her actions. If your boss asked you to pick him or her up from the airport at 5:00 A.M., would you stay out late the night before? To do so might be irresponsible. If you overslept and showed up two hours late, your boss would not trust you to work on your own.

Proving Responsibility   From your very first day on the job, show everyone with whom you work that you are reliable and trustworthy by

- Showing up and delivering your work on time.
- Always doing your best.
- Being honest and keeping your promises.
- Considering the effects of your actions on others.
- Thinking of your responsibilities first.

Being Accountable

To be **accountable** for an action, a person, or thing means that you will be responsible for it no matter what happens. When you went driving by yourself for the first time, you were accountable for the car and for your actions as a driver. If the car had been scratched, you would have been the one to answer for it.

It's the same with decisions in your career and life. Sometimes we make wrong decisions or we get blindsided by an event we can't control. Even if such accidents aren't our fault, they are our responsibility, and we have to be accountable. We need to make the best of circumstances, change the things we can control, and move on. We can't pass the buck, blame others, or ignore our responsibilities. When employers trust that you can handle the responsibility you have, they will grant you even greater responsibility.

Taking Initiative

The leaders of companies don't get to the positions of responsibility they are in by waiting for someone to tell them how to make a business run well. These men and women take initiative. Taking initiative is all about making decisions. When you take initiative, you decide to act. You assess a situation, decide what you need to do and how it needs to be done, and you do it. The leaders of companies have many people depending on them. They have to take initiative and make excellent decisions.

What Makes for an Excellent Decision?

An excellent decision is independent, informed, and responsible.

- An independent decision is one you make on your own.
- A responsible decision takes into consideration how your actions will affect others.
- An informed decision is a decision based on information instead of guesses.

The Decision-Making Process

The decision-making process usually requires three steps:

- Define your decision and determine options.
- Weigh your options.
- Consider other factors.

Defining Your Decision and Determining Options

The first step involves defining your decision. This means understanding the situation at hand and knowing what your options are. An option is a choice that you can decide for or against. Your options depend on the situation and should be choices that are realistic and doable. Here's how it works:

Part One: Defining Your Decision   First, you analyze the situation. For example, it's Friday night; you have finished work and have no plans. Next, you ask yourself exactly what you are trying to decide: what you want, what you need, or what to do. Then, you put together your question and the situation to come up with what you are trying to decide. It's Friday night, I have finished work, and I have no plans. I am trying to decide what to do.

Part Two: Determining Your Options   Start with your decision from Part One (I am trying to decide what to do). Next, brainstorm a list of as many options as you can come up with. Your list may include going to a movie, bungee jumping, cooking a nice dinner, getting on a flight to Paris. Finally, pick the options that are the most realistic and doable.

Going to a Movie	Cooking a Nice Dinner
Pro	*Pro*
Can See New Movie	Will Cost Less than $15
Can Go with Friends	Can Try New Recipe
Con	*Con*
Can't Chat in Theater	Have to Stop at the Store
Will Cost $15	Will Have to do Dishes

Dr. Joe Pace
THE EASY CHOICE

"When you are weighing your options, remember: the easy choice is not always the best choice."

Part Three: Weighing Your Options   When you weigh your options, you consider each option against your decision (*see* figure above). You then pick the option that makes the most sense for your decision. You can weigh your options by making a list of pros and cons for each option and then comparing. A pro is a positive point or benefit of an option. A con is a negative point or drawback of an option. This is what your pro and con list will look like for going to a movie and cooking a nice dinner.

Part Four: Considering Other Factors   The last step in the decision-making process is to consider other factors affecting your decision. The factors involved in a decision are the limits or boundaries that you have to work within. You can figure out the factors that affect your decision by asking a question for each pro and con. You may ask, "Do I have time to see a film or go to the store?" or "Do I have $15 to go to the movie?" That makes the decision for you. If you do not have the budget to go to a movie, it is no longer an option. Your best option becomes cooking a nice meal.

Yes You Can

Trying to decide if you should make your own decision is a decision in itself. Ask yourself, **"Can I make this decision on my own?"**

- Do I have all the information I need to make this decision?
- Am I prepared to be responsible for this decision?

Asking Questions

You can be sure you have all the information you need to make a decision by being informed. Use the knowledge-building skills you learned in Section 1.1: Either do your homework or ask. You shouldn't be afraid to ask questions, but the key to making independent decisions is gathering as much information as you can by yourself. You don't want to distract your colleagues by constantly asking their opinion, but you don't want to make an uninformed decision either. See the question scale in Figure 1.4. The rule of thumb is: If you can find the information you need on your own, then don't ask.

Training Wheels

If you are not sure if you are ready to take responsibility for your individual decisions, start slowly. Here's how:

1. Go through the decision-making process, find the best option, and choose it.
2. Present the decision you are trying to make, your options, and your decision factors to your supervisor.

Tips From a Mentor

Ten Questions you Should Ask Your Supervisor When Making a Decision or Getting an Assignment.

- *What is this for?*

- *Why am I doing this?*

- *What is the deadline for completing this assignment?*

- *How would you like me to deliver my work: via e-mail, on disc, or printed?*

- *Is there anyone I should talk to about this?*

- *Where is the best place to find research for this project?*

- *Are there any budget factors I should be aware of?*

- *Do you have any length requirements for document, presentation, and so forth?*

- *How should I format this work: as a file, report, or letter?*

- *Is there anything else I should know?*

Figure 1.4 *Question Scale*

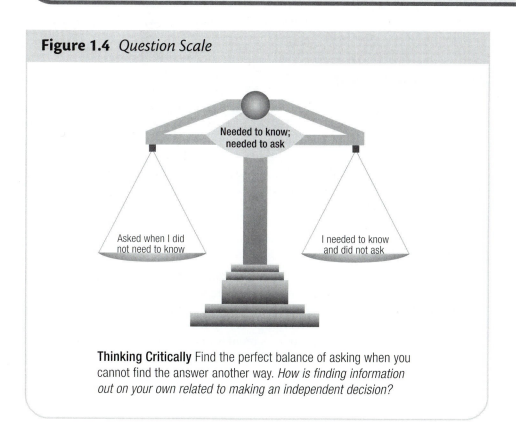

Needed to know; needed to ask

Asked when I did not need to know

I needed to know and did not ask

Thinking Critically Find the perfect balance of asking when you cannot find the answer another way. *How is finding information out on your own related to making an independent decision?*

Taking Initiative

Your Challenge

You have just become an administrative assistant. You like it so far but are starting to get restless. Your boss has been so busy writing a sales report he hasn't had time to give you any new assignments. You have already finished the work he gave you and you need something to do. What do you do?

The Possibilities

A. Spend the afternoon sending e-mails to friends and playing solitaire.

B. Clean out your desk, update your address book, order office supplies, and plan something to do tomorrow.

C. Ask your boss how you can help him prepare his sales report.

D. Interrupt your boss to ask him what you should be doing because you are getting bored.

Your Solution

Choose the solution that you think will be most effective and write a few sentences explaining your opinion. Then check your answer with the answer on our Web site: **www.mhhe.com/pace.**

3. Give your supervisor your recommendation for the best option and be prepared to say why.
4. Ask for your supervisor's advice and approval of your decision.

With this method, you are still the decision maker, but you share responsibility for approving the decision with your supervisor. It's like having training wheels as you are learning to ride a bike. Once you find your balance, you can take off the wheels and ride on your own.

Analyze Your Situation

When you take initiative and make decisions, you are finding ways to make work easier for you and your colleagues. The assignments you get on the job aren't given to you just to keep you busy. The things you do serve a purpose. Photocopying and stapling hundreds of reports for a meeting may seem like a pointless job, but it's not. The photocopies you are making will help the people at the meeting make better decisions. Part of taking initiative is recognizing the value of doing little jobs in preparation for bigger assignments.

Using Your Judgment

At some point in the decision-making process you have to act. You may never have all the information or predict all the possible outcomes of your decisions. Use your best judgment. Using your judgment is part of analyzing a situation and making a decision. In the end, your decision is based on what you judge to be the best option under the circumstances. Using your judgment is finding the fine line between common sense and assumption. If you know that you have found out everything you can, weighed your options, and are prepared to be accountable for your decision, then you have made the best decision possible.

Figure 1.5 *Putting It Together*

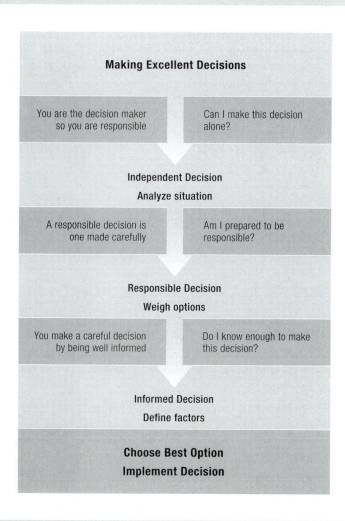

Making Excellent Decisions

You are the decision maker so you are responsible | Can I make this decision alone?

Independent Decision
Analyze situation

A responsible decision is one made carefully | Am I prepared to be responsible?

Responsible Decision
Weigh options

You make a careful decision by being well informed | Do I know enough to make this decision?

Informed Decision
Define factors

Choose Best Option
Implement Decision

Snapshot

Using your judgment is important when you have to make quick decisions. Many business decisions happen under pressure. This means you have to think on your feet. Take a snapshot, or a mental picture, of a situation to make a quick decision. Ask yourself

- **The Facts**
  What do I know? What are my options?
- **Your Main Concern**
  What do I need to decide right now? What can wait?
- **What to Ask**
  What do I need to know and what can I find out fast?

Then, do it. Make the decision, remember why, and reexamine it when you have time. If you practice your decision-making skills, you will be able to think on your feet and make excellent decisions under pressure.

Implementing Decisions

implement to put into effect

As you can see from Figure 1.5, the final step to a decision is to implement it. When you are responsible for making decisions, you are also responsible for implementing them. To **implement** a decision is to make it happen. This takes follow-through.

To get the approvals you need, you may have to persuade your superiors that your decision is an excellent one. To *persuade* is to convince someone of your point of view using reasoning. The best way to be persuasive is to be honest. Explain what you've decided and the reasons why, and then ask for help. Explain all the steps you took to make your decision. When you explain your reasoning, demonstrate that you have been thorough in your thinking and have made an excellent decision.

QUICK RECAP 1.2

BE RESPONSIBLE, TAKE INITIATIVE, MAKE DECISIONS

Let's look at what you learned in this section.
- To move forward in your career, you need to take initiative, ask questions, and be responsible.
- Being responsible means being reliable and trustworthy, as well as being accountable.
- An excellent decision is a combination of an independent decision, a responsible decision, and an informed decision.
- Decision making happens in three steps: defining your decision and determining your options, weighing your options, and considering factors.
- When you take initiative, you should analyze a situation and find ways to make your job and your colleague's jobs easier.
- When you make decisions, you need to ask if you can make the decision on your own and use your judgment to determine the answer.
- The best way to persuade people to help implement your decision is to explain your decision.

CHECK YOURSELF

1. What are the three factors that make an excellent decision?
2. When should you ask questions?

Check your answers online at **www.mhhe.com/pace.**

BUSINESS VOCABULARY

accountable responsible or answerable for a person, action, or thing
implement to put into effect
reliable dependable
responsible (1) to be reliable and trustworthy and concerned for your responsibilities; (2) to be accountable or answerable for actions, jobs, people, or things
take initiative to act of your own accord

Be Precise

To be precise means to be accurate and careful about what you do and say. Your written work can never be excellent if it is filled with inaccurate information or typos. These may seem like little mistakes, but little mistakes can create major problems, especially if the work you do is going to affect the decisions of others. In the same way that you have to be informed when you make decisions, you have to make sure that the information you provide to others is accurate. If your work is not precise, you will be responsible for any problems that arise.

The Power of the Presentation   Since you are responsible for your work, that work is a reflection of you. If your work is sloppy, it reflects badly on you. You would not walk into a job interview in jeans and a ripped shirt, because how you present yourself matters. If you look sloppy, people will think your work will be sloppy. You want to build a reputation for excellence so your colleagues will come to you when they want a job done right. You can build this reputation by being precise in everything you do.

Quality Control

Maintaining a standard of excellence is a form of **quality control.** Quality refers to the degree of excellence of a process or product. Quality is necessary in all aspects of business, from the products that a company makes, to the work that employees do. No business will succeed if their products are low in quality. The same goes for the work that their employees do. The measure of quality is how well an item or product performs its intended function, or serves its intended purpose (see Figure 1.6).

Sound Off   If you buy a stereo that skips CDs or breaks all the time, it is not performing its intended function. This means the product is of low quality. If you have to write a report explaining sales figures and you write 10 pages without actually giving an explanation, your report doesn't serve its purpose. To produce high-quality work, you have to make sure that your work performs its function or serves its purpose well.

Being Thorough

You can ensure that your work serves its purpose by being thorough. Being thorough means being careful and complete in your work. On TV crime dramas, the police are always promising a "thorough investigation." This means that they will not overlook any detail to help them solve the crime. A detail is a small part or element of a whole. In a criminal investigation, the details are clues, instructions, or information that affects an agreement, decision, action, or thing. If you say to a friend, "I would love to have lunch next week; call me tonight and we can work out the details," the "details" are the time and place. You need to pay attention to all the details in order to be thorough and ensure quality.

Reading and Study Tip

Building Ideas
Think about how this section is structured. How do the ideas build on one another?

> ❝ *We are what we repeatedly do. Excellence, therefore, is not an act, but a habit.* ❞
>
> *Aristotle*
> *Ancient Greek Philosopher and Scientist*

quality control a specific strategy to ensure quality

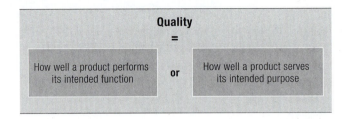

Figure 1.6 *Measure of Quality*

Thinking Critically People rate the quality of an item on how well it performs. *How would this method of measuring quality apply to an employee?*

Paying Attention to Detail

To pay attention to detail means taking into account the specifics or smaller parts of an idea or project. When you pay attention to detail, you consider every part of what you are doing, instead of just the main idea or thing. There is no such thing as a minor detail because all details affect the overall quality of a piece of work. Getting a single detail wrong can have major consequences. If you forget one detail when calculating your income taxes, for example, you could end up owing the IRS a lot of money.

Content and Presentation

When it comes to written work, you should pay attention to detail in two areas: content and presentation. Content is the information or ideas in the text. Presentation is how the work and its contents are presented or shown. For example, Figure 1.7 shows two e-mails announcing a company picnic. One was written by a person who was not precise about content or presentation; the other was written by someone who was more thorough.

Fact Checking Content

When you fact check content, you review the important details to make sure they are all included and are accurate. You need to check the content of your work thoroughly to make sure that

1. **You included the complete information you need for your work to serve its purpose.** Here's *how:*
   - Isolate the purpose of your work. *Example:* The purpose of the e-mail is to announce the picnic and invite the marketing department.
   - Find out what you need to include for your work to serve its purpose. *Example:* Ask yourself, what do people need to know to be able to come to this picnic?
   - Apply the five Ws—who, what, why, where, and when—to make sure you've covered all the important information. *Example:*
     - Who's the announcement for? The Marketing Department
     - What is the announcement about? The Company Picnic.
     - Why are they having it? To celebrate Employee Appreciation Day
     - Where is it? South Park Field
     - When? This Saturday from 4–6:00 pm

Figure 1.7 *Precise Content and Presentation*   21

Mail

Send | Save Draft | Attach | Tools | Cancel

To: Marketing Department

Cc:

Bcc:

Subject: picnick

Come join us Saterday starting after 3.
Everyone invited for food and fun!
Please RSVP to Maggie and with how many people.
Picnick depends on weather.

Example 1

Mail

Send | Save Draft | Attach | Tools | Cancel

To: Marketing Department

Cc:

Bcc:

Subject: Company Picnic to Celebrate Employee Appreciation Day

This Saturday from 4:00-6:00 pm at South Park Field.
Join your colleagues for the company picnic!
There will be dinner, fun activities for kids, and softball for adults!
Please RSVP to Maggie on extension 24 with the number of people
you will bring.
Directions will be posted on the office notice board.
We will notify you by e-mail if the picnic is rescheduled due to rain.

Example 2

Thinking Critically Both content and presentation are important in communications. *What was included in Example 2 that makes it more precise than Example 1?*

2. **Your facts and figures are accurate.** Here's *how:*
   - Isolate the important facts and figures in your work. *Example:* The facts are the picnic is from 4–6:00 pm at South Park Field; families are welcome; there will be activities; directions will be on boards; RSVP to Maggie; Maggie's extension is 24; there will be another location if it rains.
   - Confirm that these facts are correct by consulting with someone who knows or by looking them up in the appropriate resource.

Pace Points

Thoroughly Precise
Being thorough means check, double-check, and have a partner triple-check for precision.

3. **Your main ideas and statements are clear and easy to understand.** Here's *how:*
   - Isolate the ideas and statements in your work. *Example:* The main idea is that everyone in the marketing department is invited to a picnic.
   - Make sure they are clearly explained and easily understood.

Proofreading

When you proofread, you thoroughly examine your work to ensure that you do not overlook details that will affect presentation (*see* Figure 1.8). When you proofread, you are looking at three specific things:

1. **Well-organized information.**
   - Give work a heading, including a title and date.
   - Separate important information from main text, using bold letters or separate headers.
   - Number pages for reports and long letters.
   - Use labeled dividers to separate sections or chapters; create a table of contents or an index to access important subjects immediately.
2. **Correct spelling, grammar, and vocabulary.**
   - Make sure to use the appropriate word to explain an idea; look up unfamiliar words before using them.
   - Use spelling and grammar checkers when working on word processing programs.
   - Print out and read work for spelling and grammar in addition to using spell check software.
3. **Polished work.**
   - Type work so it is neater, is easier to read, and looks professional.
   - Check for typos when working on a computer.
   - Present work on clean white paper without pencil marks, doodles, coffee stains, or whiteout.
   - Present reports in binders and memos in files; type addresses neatly to polish finished work.

Figure 1.8 *Being Thorough*

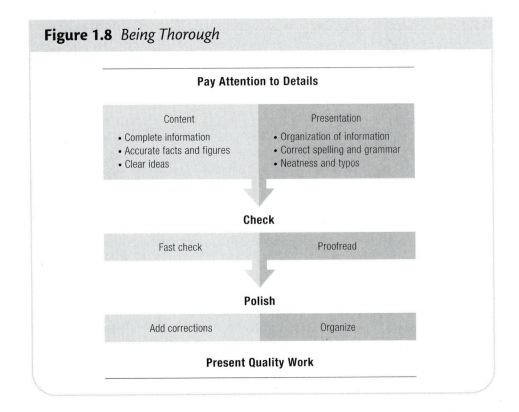

New Attitudes / New Opportunities

Meet Garrett White. Garrett is originally from Texas but was raised in Cleveland, Ohio. He now works in finance for General Electric. He is also involved in GE's six-sigma program, which he explains is a set of tools used to ensure quality at GE. Here's what Garrett has to tell us about . . .

Why He Has to Be Precise In His Job and Why That Is Important   "At GE, I currently work in a finance function and within finance we report results and do estimates. So everything is about being precise, accurate, and on time. I've had a lot of practice in that. I started off as a pricing analyst where we did reports that management used to make huge commercial decisions. It's important to be precise because without precision and accuracy, you are prone to make mistakes. Then when your reports get to higher management, they have bad data and thus make a wrong decision that may cost a lot of people their jobs."

What It Means to Him to Pay Attention to Detail   "To pay attention to detail in my job is to do it, check it, do it again, check it again, take your eyes away from it, and have somebody else check it. Anytime there's a manual touch point, there's an opportunity for human error. I consistently check and cross-check my work to make sure it's accurate."

When, How, and Why You Should Correct Mistakes   "When is immediately. How is, if your report has been communicated to others, let that person know immediately what the error is, what it means, and what the implications are of that error. Then let them know what the correction is. Always remember that what you turn in is a reflection of you. You can look at a fax that somebody sends and if it's really sloppy, it reflects on the person that sent it. People need to be able to trust your work. If you turn something in and somebody's always second guessing it, then you as an employee begin to lose value. Quality means making sure your work is presentable, as well as making sure it is correct."

Going the Extra Mile

When we are precise, we are accurate and get things right the first time. However, all people make mistakes. Being thorough and paying attention to detail will help you catch mistakes and correct them before you turn in your work. However, if you find a mistake after you hand in your work, you need to go the extra mile to correct it before it causes problems.

Right Now

Mistakes get worse the longer they are left uncorrected. If you spot a mistake, do whatever it takes to correct it immediately. Make it right, NOW:

- **N** Notify people of the mistake.
- **O** Outline steps to correct it.
- **W** Work to fix the mistake.

It's easier to correct a mistake right away than if you wait. The longer you leave a mistake, the more the mistake multiplies as people pass along incorrect data. It will save you time and energy to own up to your mistake and correct it as soon as possible.

> *Pace Points*
>
> **Be Consistent**
>
> Prevent confusion or outdated material by making changes the same way each time. If you make a change, correction, or improvement to a file on your computer, do it for the files on your share drive and the files in your drawers.

Mistakes Are Everyone's Responsibility

Even if you didn't make the mistake, it is your responsibility to correct it. Mistakes are everyone's responsibility because mistakes affect everyone. If you are filing and you notice other files in the wrong place, do you just leave them there? If you are precise, you take the five extra minutes to fix the files. It benefits you to go the extra mile to correct this mistake because you may need those files later. If you leave them in the wrong place, it will take twice as long to find them again than it would to simply put them in their proper place. Leaving mistakes for others to deal with is irresponsible. There is no guarantee that a mistake will be noticed or corrected. Making an honest mistake is excusable; intentionally ignoring a mistake is not.

Do It Right the First Time

You can avoid spending time and energy correcting mistakes, if you do a good job the first time. By now, you should know that it's easier to do a job right the first time than it is to go back and fix it later. Did you ever leave dinner dishes to "soak" instead of washing them? Instead of just washing them and being done, the dishes sit in dirty water for hours and you end up doing twice the work to get them clean. The same goes for your work. If you cut corners and do a half-hearted job, you will inevitably have to go back to correct mistakes. Be precise and be thorough. The time you spend doing a job right is time you save correcting mistakes.

Being Helpful

Notice a pattern here? A little time spent going the extra mile saves you time in other ways. The same rule applies to helping people. If someone has a question or needs a hand, whether it's a colleague or a customer, it takes very little for you to help them. Ten minutes of help lasts a lifetime as gratitude. Even if it's not your job, it is always your responsibility to do what you can to help people. If the positions were reversed, you would want someone to go the extra mile for you. You are responsible for the work you do and the impression it leaves with other people. Your work also represents your company. If you do poor work, it reflects poorly on you and your company. If you do precise, excellent work, your colleagues and customers will think of you as a true professional and an asset to any organization.

QUICK RECAP 1.3

BE PRECISE

In this section you found out about
- The importance of being precise.
- Quality control and how quality is measured.
- How being thorough and paying attention to detail will help you to ensure high quality.
- How to be thorough in your content and presentation by fact checking and proofreading.
- When and how to correct mistakes and avoid them by doing the job right the first time.
- The importance of going the extra mile to help others.

CHECK YOURSELF

1. What determines the quality of a product?
2. How can you avoid going back to correct mistakes when you do a job?

Check your answers online at **www.mhhe.com/pace.**

BUSINESS VOCABULARY

quality control   a specific strategy to ensure quality

Develop Personal and Professional Ethics

When you are at work, do you help yourself to office supplies to use at home? Do you make long-distance calls to friends on your office phone? Do you use company resources for your personal gain? Of course you don't, because you are an ethical person. **Ethics** is a system of morals that helps you determine right from wrong. A personal standard of excellence requires ethics so that you will not only make the smart choice, but also the right choice.

Do the Right Thing We may have laws and rules to guide us, but sometimes it's up to us to decide what's right. Whatever your upbringing, religion, culture, or race, you have grown up with a notion of what it means to do the right thing. Every culture teaches the Golden Rule: Treat other people the way we want to be treated. Don't lie if you don't want to be lied to, and don't steal if you don't want to be stolen from. This rule will help you both to understand the kind of ethical behavior your employers expect from you and to know the ethical behavior you can expect from them.

Reading and Study Tip

Compound Sentences
A compound sentence is a sentence in two parts joined by *and* or *but.* Look for examples of compound sentences as you read.

ethics a system of morals and behavior

❝ *Rather fail with honor, than succeed by fraud.* ❞

Sophocles
Ancient Greek Philosopher and Playwright

Personal Ethics

Personal ethics is your individual understanding of right and wrong. Everyone will look at the same situation with slightly different eyes depending on his or her personal ethics. Morals are not enough. When you have ethics, you know the right thing to do, and you do it.

Honesty Pays

Business managers do not want to spend time and money monitoring the behavior of their employees. They need to trust that their employees will behave honestly and ethically. You already know that to succeed in business you need to be trustworthy and reliable. This means you tell the truth and do not lie, cheat, or steal. You can demonstrate your personal ethics by being honest both on the job and in your job.

Being honest *on* the job means

- Using company resources such as phone lines, faxes, and e-mail for business only.
- Putting only genuine business expenses on company credit cards and expense reports.
- Being truthful about the hours you work when filling time sheets.
- Being truthful about absences due to illness.
- Being truthful about your past employment history and/or criminal record.

Being honest *in* your job means

- Turning in and taking credit for only your own work.
- Not lying or manipulating facts for your own purposes.
- Keeping confidential documents and information private.

- Being honest about your colleagues when reporting to superiors.
- Using legal and genuine information and services to do your work.

Dishonest employees can cost companies a lot of money. Long-distance calls and office supplies add up. Honest employees know this and do not misuse the resources their employers provide to help them do their job. Successful professionals are honest and can be trusted to use company money wisely.

Work Ethic

Having a work ethic is an important part of having personal ethics. A **work ethic** is the sense of duty that you bring to your work. When you accept a job, you accept certain responsibilities. Your employer will expect you to

- Show up for work.
- Be on time.
- Do your work to the best of your ability.
- Be loyal to your company.
- Follow company rules and directions from superiors.
- Obey local and federal law.
- Do your work unimpaired by drugs or alcohol.
- Follow safety precautions and consider the safety of others.
- Work in a professional, nonviolent way with co-workers and customers.

If you do not meet these expectations, you are being negligent as an employee. To be **negligent** means to be indifferent, careless, or casual about your duties. Negligence on the job can be worse than being dishonest. If a banker or accountant lies, people will lose money, but if a safety inspector is negligent, people can get hurt or even killed.

work ethic the sense of duty that you bring to your work

negligent indifferent, careless, or casual about duties

Professional Ethics

The decisions you make have consequences that affect not only you, but also other people in your life. That's why you make ethical decisions. Corporate decision-makers have an even greater obligation to make ethical decisions because their decisions affect

- Workers
- Customers
- Suppliers
- Shareholders
- Consumers
- Community

In order to do right by all of the people that depend on them, business leaders need to have professional ethics. Professional ethics are the standards of right and wrong that businesses follow. There are specific professional ethics for different professions, but all professional ethics consider the impact and morality of business decisions.

Professional Ethics in the Global Community

Globalization is the opening up of the markets of the world to allow countries to freely trade goods, services, labor, and capital. Because of advances in communication and transportation, globalization is happening faster than ever. In today's

globalization the opening up of world markets to allow countries to freely trade goods, services, labor, and capital

global community, business decisions impact the world. Ethical businesses respect the environment by

- Ensuring products and factories don't pollute the environment.
- Ensuring construction doesn't destroy land or harm wildlife.
- Ensuring natural resources and energy are conserved.
- Ensuring industrial waste is disposed of in an environmentally safe way.
- Prohibiting animals from being subjected to unethical testing.

They respect human rights by

- Paying fair wages to workers in all countries.
- Prohibiting child labor, forced labor, or exploitation.
- Preventing discrimination or harassment in any form.
- Providing a minimum wage for employees.
- Allowing workers to join unions.

They respect health and safety by

- Providing safe and healthy working conditions.
- Guaranteeing fair work hours with time off.
- Providing health resources for full-time employees.
- Being responsible for the safety of consumer products.
- Ensuring the business contributes to the health safety of its community.

They respect the law and contracts by

- Operating a legal business.
- Reporting financial information accurately and on time.
- Keeping employee records and information private.
- Honoring obligations to employees, customers, suppliers, and shareholders.
- Providing pension or retirement savings options for full-time employees.

Codes of Conduct

Corporate codes of conduct are a way for individual companies to formally state the personal ethics they expect from their employees and the professional ethics their employees can expect of them. Codes of conduct respect local law and federal regulations, but they also go further by stating the specific way the company practices professional ethics.

Using the Code

The law does not require companies to publish a code of conduct, but company leaders see the benefit of having their ethical policies formalized. Codes of conduct tell employees what is expected of them in order to limit the responsibility, or **liability,** of the company should an employee violate the code. However, codes of conduct are useless unless they are upheld. To uphold a code of conduct, all employees should read their company's code in order to know

- What the company considers to be acceptable conduct.
- What the company considers to be misconduct.
- How to deal with and report misconduct.
- What the penalties are for misconduct.

liability area of potential legal responsibility

In some situations, it may be hard to know the correct and ethical course of action. Use your company's code of conduct to help you make the right choice.

Misconduct

In most companies, **misconduct** is considered a knowing and deliberate act of unethical or illegal behavior. If someone commits misconduct, he or she is doing something he or she knows is wrong.

misconduct knowing and deliberate act of unethical or illegal behavior

Dealing with Misconduct

The punishment for misconduct varies from company to company. Possible consequences of misconduct are

- Monetary fines.
- Required education programs.
- Demotion or loss of privileges.
- Probation or suspension.
- Dismissal.
- Jail.

How misconduct is dealt with depends on these factors:

- Seriousness of the offense.
- Position of the parties involved.
- Frequency of offense.
- Exceptional circumstances.

For example, if an adult office worker is caught having an alcoholic beverage at lunch, it is not as serious an offense as a school bus driver doing the same thing.

How Do You Know?

Like all questions of right and wrong, questions of misconduct can be murky at times. You may think that misconduct has occurred, but you need to be sure before you make a formal accusation. When accusations of misconduct arise, the accuser bears the burden of proof. This means that it is up to the person making the accusation to prove that misconduct occurred. If you believe misconduct is occurring, ask the five Ws—who, what, why, where, and when—to establish the facts of the situation.

Reasonable Explanation

If you suspect misconduct, the first step you should take is to look for a reasonable explanation. Let's use the example of missing office supplies. You do the ordering for your office and you notice that a lot of items are missing.

1. **Assess what you know.**
   Look for a reasonable explanation. Mention to your colleagues that they are going through supplies too fast and ask why without making any accusations.
   - **Best-Case Scenario**
     If there is no misconduct, your search should result in a legitimate explanation.
   - **Second-Best Scenario**
     If there is no explanation, your questions will warn whoever is taking the supplies that you are aware of the misconduct. This should discourage any more theft.

2. Take preventative action.

If you can't find an explanation and the problem continues, then take steps to prevent it. Notify everyone of the problem and keep valuables locked up.

Reporting Misconduct

Before you report misconduct, make sure you have evidence to prove your accusation. Evidence is confirmation of a crime or misconduct. Types of evidence include

- Documents.
- Witness testimony.
- Samples of negligent work.
- Surveillance video.
- Physical evidence from fingerprinting or drug tests.

Start by filing a complaint with your immediate superior. If this person is involved, then report to his or her superior. Many human resources departments have employees who investigate complaints or anonymous hotlines for reporting misconduct. These are also options for filing accusations of misconduct. If the misconduct involves people in a position of power, you can seek help in reporting the misconduct from outside sources. There are lawyers and business bureaus that specialize in maintaining ethical business practices. Any kind of accusation is very serious and can do lasting damage to reputations and working relationships. It is unethical to make false accusations of misconduct for any reason.

Internet Quest

Know the Law

Look up "white-collar crime" in a search engine. Find a definition and examples of this kind of crime. Words to look for: embezzlement, profiteering, industrial espionage, conflict of interest, and insider trading.

Harassment

harassment any form of constant torment or bothersome behavior that singles out an individual in an uncomfortable or upsetting way

Harassment is any form of constant, bothersome behavior that singles out an individual in an uncomfortable or upsetting way. This includes

- Making racial slurs.
- Displaying explicit or provocative material in your office.
- Making fun of someone's physical appearance.
- Making unwanted physical contact or advances.
- Threatening or bullying.
- Making jokes that endanger or embarrass people.
- Singling people out because of their race, religion, gender, sexual orientation, physical appearance, or any other personal quality.

Going Too Far

Friendly joking is fine, but it can go too far if you single out a person and cause that person to feel uncomfortable or embarrassed. The problem is that different people have different levels of sensitivity. An innocent joke or e-mail that is funny to you may be offensive to someone else. There is no way to know if someone is laughing with you or simply because they think they have to. Feeling forced to do something that makes you uncomfortable is the definition of harassment.

Dealing with Harassment

Give people the benefit of the doubt. If someone says something thoughtless that upsets you, it is not harassment. If they do it repeatedly, then you need

Tips From a Mentor

No Offense

To avoid offending someone, don't get too personal at work. Here are ten things you can do to avoid harassment or perceived harassment at work:

- **Don't forward e-mail jokes, chain letters, political petitions,** or nonwork-related messages. Even if you just forward an e-mail, you are considered responsible for it also.

- **Don't display** political, religious, or very personal material in your workspace. Photos of you and/or your family or loved ones are fine.

- **Don't make assumptions.** Don't assume everyone celebrates a holiday, shares an opinion, or lives a certain lifestyle.

- **Don't promote stereotyping** by assuming a person has skills, preferences, or knowledge because of his or her race, religion, gender, or sexual orientation.

- **Limit physical contact** to a handshake. Respect personal space.

- **Compliment people** on their work, not their appearances.

- **Dress appropriately.** Wearing revealing clothes can make others uncomfortable.

- **Avoid very personal conversations at work.** Work is not the time to discuss your medical problems, your love life, your finances, or your political and religious views.

- **Don't listen to provocative radio** or music at work.

- **Don't ask co-workers out at the office.** It creates an awkward and uncomfortable situation if the person is not interested.

to do something. There are three steps to dealing with harassment: ask, tell, and warn.

- Approach the person who is upsetting you. Inform that person that his or her behavior is upsetting you and calmly and politely ASK him or her to stop.
- If the behavior doesn't stop, use stronger language and TELL him or her that the behavior has to stop.
- If the behavior continues, then WARN the person that you will file an official complaint if he or she doesn't stop immediately.

If you do file a complaint, be sure to follow the same guidelines for making a misconduct report.

DEVELOP PERSONAL AND PROFESSIONAL ETHICS

Here's what you learned about personal and professional ethics:
- Ethics is a system of morals that helps you determine right from wrong.
- Making ethical decisions involves doing the right thing and treating others the way you want to be treated.
- Professional ethics concerns the responsibilities of both employees and the companies they work for.
- In the age of globalization, companies have a greater responsibility to practice professional ethics because their decisions affect the global community.
- Codes of conduct are a way for companies to state what employees can expect of them and what they expect of employees.
- A code of conduct serves as a guide for dealing with misconduct.
- Misconduct is intentional unethical behavior.

CHECK YOURSELF

1. What does it mean to do the right thing?
2. How can you avoid being accused of harassment?

Check your answers online at **www.mhhe.com/pace.**

BUSINESS VOCABULARY

ethics   a system of morals and behavior

globalization   the opening up of world markets to allow countries to freely trade goods, services, labor, and capital

harassment   any form of constant torment or bothersome behavior that singles out an individual in an uncomfortable or upsetting way

liability   area of potential legal responsibility

misconduct   knowing and deliberate act of unethical or illegal behavior

negligent   indifferent, careless, or casual about duties

Take Pride in Your Work

If you are ever around children, you know how proud they are when they come home from school with an A on a paper. The first thing they do is write their name in the corner and hang their work on the fridge. In business, you are not going to come home from work eager to display your file or report, but you will have that same feeling of pride when you do a good job. This is the reward for doing hard work. You will look at your finished accomplishment, smile, and feel good that you lived up to your own high standard of excellence.

Your Standards   By becoming well informed, being responsible, taking initiative, making decisions, being precise, and developing your personal and professional ethics, you set your own standard of excellence. By taking pride in your work, caring about what you do and how you do it, you will be motivated to live up to your own standard of excellence.

Take Ownership of Your Work

Just as children put their names on their schoolwork before they hang it up, you want your name stamped on all the work you do. In some cases, you won't actually write your name on a report or project, but by making all the work the same high quality, you put your mark of excellence on it.

Your Standard, Your Name

If you always deliver high-quality, well-presented, precise work, whoever receives it will come to recognize it as yours. It will have your name written all over it. When you start out in business, you won't always get a chance to do individual work or be able to take credit for a project. In business, we often **collaborate,** or work together with others. However, your supervisors and managers can recognize your unique standard of excellence and your contribution to the whole project. In this way, you can build a reputation for excellence.

Professional Reputation

You want your name to be associated with excellent work. If you never spell-check and you hand in assignments full of typos and spelling mistakes, your poor spelling is what your superiors will remember. You make a first impression when you meet someone. The same applies when someone reviews your work for the first time. Make a good impression by maintaining a standard of excellence so that everything you do is of the highest quality. When you keep a high standard, your name will be associated with high quality. This kind of positive professional recognition is how you can move ahead in the business world. By building a reputation for delivering consistently high-quality work, you will be trusted to handle bigger and more challenging assignments.

> **Reading and Study Tip**
>
> ***Cause and Effect***
> Our actions always cause something else to happen. Find three examples of cause and effect in this section.

collaborate work together

Dr. Joe Pace
ATTITUDE

"The pleasure you get from your life is equal to the attitude you put into it."

Earning Respect

incentive a reward or source of motivation

motivation what drives us to act

One of the best things about doing good work is earning your colleagues' respect and approval. Confirmation that we did good work gives us incentive to keep doing good work. An **incentive** is a reward or source of motivation. **Motivation** is what causes us to act.

Polite Pride   Part of taking pride in your work is accepting compliments and approval graciously. If someone says, "Great job on that project," say, "Thank you, I'm glad it was helpful." You don't have to be shy; if you did a great job, accept the recognition you deserve. After all, those compliments inspire you to keep doing good work. Be proud of what you've done, but never stop trying to do better.

It's Up to You

We all want to be appreciated for what we do, and doing high-quality work is one way to earn that appreciation. You are responsible for deciding what quality of work you will do, setting a high standard, and using the tools you learned to live up to that standard.

Policing Yourself

If you want to succeed in the business world, you have to constantly try to improve the quality of your work. If you work to build a reputation as someone with a high standard of excellence but then begin to do poor-quality work, you will lose your reputation. You have probably already figured out in life that there are talkers and doers. The *talkers* are people who tell you all their big plans and accomplishments but never quite deliver. The *doers* are people who let their actions and the high quality of the results do the talking for them. To keep from being just a talker, make sure that you don't let your standards slip. If your reputation is built on excellent work, then that's what you have to do every time to maintain your reputation. Let your excellent work do the talking for you.

Discipline

discipline strict control that enforces compliance

compliance to obey

Living up to a high standard takes discipline. **Discipline** means a strict control that enforces compliance. **Compliance** means to obey. If you are on a diet and you walk by a donut shop, it takes a lot of self-discipline not to walk in and order a couple of jellies. The same goes for living up to your own standards. You may get stressed or tired and decide to cut corners on a project. If you are overworked, get help on a project, but don't turn in something of low quality. It is much harder to rebuild your reputation after your standards slip than to make sure they don't slip at all. Just as with donuts, it's a lot easier to walk by the store than to work off the extra calories after eating a half-dozen glazed.

Responsibility

Throughout this section, the idea of responsibility keeps appearing. You are responsible for the work you do and the quality of that work. You are accountable if your decisions are unethical or uninformed. This is a big incentive to do excellent work. If you know you are responsible for the work you do, then you are not going to do

Too Much to Do

Your Challenge

You are at your wit's end. You have two assignments due for your boss in the next week, and it seems like every five minutes people are walking by dropping more work on your desk. You have a reputation for doing really good work, so people want your help. You pride yourself on being responsible, and if you make a promise or accept a deadline, you do your best to deliver on time. At this rate, though, you don't know if you can get it all done and done well.

The Possibilities

A. Scramble to get everything done and hope you don't make mistakes.
B. Tell everyone that you can't handle any more work and they have to leave you alone.
C. Meet with your boss, explain the situation, and agree to concentrate on the most important assignment.
D. Give all the unimportant work to a temp and worry about the project that will give you the most recognition.

Your Solution

Choose the possible solution that you think will be most effective and write a few sentences explaining your opinion. Then check your answer with the answer on our Web site: **www.mhhe.com/pace**.

Pace
ONLINE

---

bad work intentionally. If you know you have done good work, you will have no problem answering for it. When you do excellent work, you can hold your head high because you have credibility and integrity.

Credibility and Integrity

To have **credibility** means you can be trusted and believed. To have **integrity** means to have pride, honor, and sincerity. You can't have one without the other. If you have strong personal and professional ethics, credibility, and a sense of responsibility, you have integrity. Integrity is something no one can take away from you but you. Integrity is knowing what you believe, what you stand for, and what kind of work you do. Having a reputation for integrity is the result of setting and keeping a standard of excellence. If you cut corners, do sloppy work, or are dishonest or negligent, then you hurt yourself by damaging your integrity. You know you have integrity when you do not compromise your standard of excellence or your ethics to get a job done. When you work with integrity, you can be proud of yourself, what you have accomplished, and what you will accomplish.

credibility trustworthiness and believability

integrity pride, honor, and sincerity

Get to Work

You are ready to get to work at building the career you have always wanted. You know how to do excellent work, make excellent decisions, and act with integrity. There is nothing stopping you from moving forward in your career. You are ready to do business as a professional.

❝ The secret joy in work is contained in one word: excellence. To know how to do something well is to enjoy it. ❞

Pearl S. Buck
American Writer and Humanitarian

TAKE PRIDE IN YOUR WORK

Here's what we discussed in this section:
- Take pride in your work.
- Take ownership in your work by putting your "name" on it.
- Build a positive professional reputation.
- Approval and appreciation are incentives.
- Accept compliments graciously.
- Stick to your own standards by being disciplined.
- You must be responsible to do excellent work.
- Stick up for your choices and correct mistakes with integrity.

CHECK YOURSELF

1. What kind of professional reputation do you want to build?
2. Who is responsible for making us stick to our standard of excellence?

Check your answers online at www.mhhe.com/pace.

BUSINESS VOCABULARY

collaborate work together
incentive a reward or source of motivation
motivation what drives us to act
discipline strict control that enforces compliance
compliance to obey
credibility trustworthiness and believability
integrity pride, honor, and sincerity

Chapter Summary

1.1 Be Well Informed

Objective: *Define and acquire the knowledge you need to be well informed and do excellent work.*

In this section, you learned that being well informed gives you the confidence to make decisions and come up with new ideas. You learned the types of knowledge that you need to develop. You also found out how you can build knowledge by doing your homework and asking questions. Being well informed is an essential part of building a standard of excellence.

1.2 Be Responsible, Take Initiative, Make Decisions

Objective: *Be responsible, take initiative, and make excellent decisions.*

In this section, you learned that in order to get into the driver's seat in your career, you have to prove to your employers that you can be responsible, take initiative, and make decisions. Taking initiative involves analyzing a situation, deciding how it can be improved, and doing it. You learned that to make an excellent decision, you have to be able to make independent, responsible, and well-informed decisions.

1.3 Be Precise

Objective: *Be precise and accurate and go the extra mile to ensure excellence in everything you do.*

This section outlined the key component of having a standard of excellence: being precise. This means being accurate in everything you do. You found out that you need to be thorough and pay attention to detail by fact checking and proofreading. You also learned that you have to go the extra mile to correct mistakes and do excellent work.

1.4 Develop Personal and Professional Ethics

Objective: *Identify your personal and professional ethics and learn how to deal with misconduct and harassment.*

In this section, you found out what it means to have personal and professional ethics. You learned why we need ethics and how it is outlined in corporate codes of conduct. You learned what you can do if you have to deal with misconduct and harassment at work.

1.5 Take Pride in Your Work

Objective: *Take pride in your work by maintaining your standard of excellence.*

This final section taught you that you can develop your own standard of excellence by bringing together all the skills you learned in Sections 1.1 through 1.4. You also found out that you are the one responsible for sticking to this standard and that that takes discipline. When you do excellent work and have integrity, you can be proud of your accomplishments.

Business Vocabulary

- accountable (p. 12)
- asset (p. 8)
- capital (p. 11)
- capitalize on (p. 11)
- collaborate (p. 33)
- compliance (p. 34)
- credibility (p. 35)
- discipline (p. 34)

- ethics (p. 26)
- globalization (p. 27)
- harassment (p. 30)
- implement (p. 17)
- incentive (p. 34)
- integrity (p. 35)
- liability (p. 28)
- misconduct (p. 29)

- motivation (p. 34)
- negligent (p. 27)
- quality control (p. 19)
- reliable (p. 12)
- responsible (p. 12)
- take initiative (p. 12)
- work ethic (p. 27)

Key Concept Review

1. What makes up common sense? (1.1)
2. What are the two types of knowledge strengths? (1.1)
3. What is the first step in the decision-making process? (1.2)
4. Who is responsible for taking initiative? (1.2)
5. Why is it important for your work to be polished and presentable? (1.3)

6. What do the five Ws stand for and when do you use them? (1.4)
7. What steps must you take in order to create quality work? (1.4)
8. What does it mean to do the right thing? (1.5)
9. What does a compliment express? (1.5)
10. What does it mean to have integrity? (1.5)

Online Project

Codes of Conduct

Look at the business section of the newspaper or watch the financial news on TV. Choose the names of three companies you recognize, such as AT&T or Wal-Mart. Type their names into a search engine and try to locate the company home pages. Once you are on the home page, try to find information on each company's corporate code of conduct.

Write a list comparing and contrasting the main points of each company's corporate code of conduct.

(Hint: Corporate codes of conduct may be referred to as *mission statements* or *compliance codes*.)

Step Up the Pace

CASE A *Foreign Visitors*

Your boss informs you that your department will be hosting three associates from your company's sister office in Japan. They are coming to stay for a week, and your boss has asked you to arrange some activities to introduce them to your local community and make them feel welcome. You also want to make sure that everyone in your office treats them with respect by being knowledgeable about their country and culture.

What to Do

1. Think about what you would do to become well informed about Japan, Japanese culture, and activities for tourists to do in your own community.
2. Write a draft of a memo you would send to the people in your office with the information you found out about Japan and its culture.

CASE B *Harassment in the Workplace*

You get along really well with everyone in your office, but you have been having problems lately with one person who keeps forwarding you joke e-mails. Most of the jokes are harmless, but a few times, you have been offended by some very tasteless and insensitive jokes. You don't want to make a huge deal about it, but you also don't want to receive these e-mails any more, and you don't think that this person should be sending them in the office.

What to Do

1. Think of the best way to address this problem so you can all get back to work.
2. Write out the steps you would take to address this problem, starting with your first step and ending with your last resort.

Correcting Misspellings

As you proofread your work, you may be unsure about how to spell some words. Spell-check on word processing programs can help, but they don't catch everything. Words that sound alike but are spelled differently (homophones) are especially troublesome. Certainly you have heard that you should look up spellings in the dictionary. The only problem is that dictionaries are organized by spelling! Here are some spelling tips:

- Use spell-check—but also proofread everything yourself.
- Use a dictionary to check if you are using the correct homophone (such as *too, to,* and *two*).
- Use an online dictionary site that offers alternative spellings. This feature makes them more useful than "hard copy" dictionaries.
- Memorize or keep by your desk a copy of the correct spellings of words you often misspell.
- Choose the autocorrect setting on your word processing program.

Choose the correct spelling for each sentence. Use a dictionary if needed.

1. I believe its/it's time to go.
2. It snowed a lot/alot last night.

The correct answer for sentence 1 is *it's*. As a contraction, you can break it down to *it is* and it still makes sense in the sentence.

For B, the correct answer is *a lot*. There is no such word as *alot*.

Exercise: Circle the correct spelling. Use a dictionary if needed.

1. calender/calendar	12. ocassion/occasion
2. definitelydefinately	13. occurrence/ocurrance
3. equipment/equiptment	14. posession/possession
4. experiense/experience	15. privilege/privalege
5. gauranty/guarantee	16. receipt/reciept
6. harassment/harasment	17. refered/referred
7. imediate/immediate	18. recommend/reccomend
8. license/lisense	19. restaurant/restarant
9. maintainance/maintenance	20. shedule/schedule
10. misspell/mispel	21. seperate/separate
11. neighbor/nieghbor	22. untill/until

The Dynamics of Effective Teamwork

What Will You Do?

2.1 The Importance of Teamwork Examine the origins of teamwork, its role in society, and its importance in business and life.

2.2 Where Teamwork Starts Learn individual skills that will prepare you to be an effective member of a team.

2.3 Organizing a Team Examine the goals, functions, and procedures of an organized team.

2.4 Negotiating and Resolving Conflict Learn how to build a working team by recognizing, resolving, and preventing conflict.

2.5 Working Effectively with Others Work as a team, making decisions, solving problems, and achieving goals.

Why Do You Need to Know This?

To be successful in today's business world, it is important to understand the value of teamwork. Teamwork has changed the way businesses operate. Today's employers know that people usually enjoy what they do, and do their jobs better, when they work as part of a team. When everyone works toward a common goal and shares ideas, resources, and responsibilities, they can accomplish more. It is not enough to just *understand* the importance of teamwork; in today's professional world, successful people also must know how to *be* effective team members. This chapter will teach you the knowledge and skills you need to be a successful team player.

Chapter Objectives

After completing this chapter, you will be able to:

- Define the role and importance of teamwork in the business world.

- Explain and use the individual skills needed to be a productive team member.

- Organize yourself and your team, identify goals, and take action.

- Identify, address, and prevent conflict among team members.

- Collaborate with teammates to solve group problems and accomplish goals successfully.

Set the *Pace*

Teamwork   Think about a time when you worked or played as part of a team. Ask yourself the following questions, and make a list of the pros and cons of that teamwork experience:

- What went well?
- What could have gone better?
- Did your team accomplish its goal?

Activity   In the experience journal section of your career portfolio, write two or three paragraphs to describe your teamwork experience and explain what you might have done to improve your team's performance. Then, share your thoughts with your classmates.

The Importance of Teamwork

Have you ever taken a subway ride at 8:00 on a Monday morning? Maybe you've taken the bus or gotten stuck in a traffic jam while people scramble and rush to get to their jobs. It's not fun. In fact, it's what most people like least about going to work in the morning. At 8:00 AM on a crowded subway, it seems as if everyone is in a hurry. It's *rush hour.* No one has any patience. If there's an empty seat on the bus, someone will grab it, even if you've been waiting longer. On the freeway, some drivers will try to move ahead by cutting off others.

The "Me-First" Attitude   Okay, the morning commute is not always that bad. It's just that the "me-first" attitude can make getting to work a nightmare. Now imagine what a nightmare it would be if you faced that same kind of attitude at your job.

Reading and Study Tip

Cause and Effect
Events are linked. One event causes another. Causes have effects. Look for cause-and-effect relationships as you read. On a separate sheet of paper, list three positive benefits of teamwork.

Teamwork in the Workplace

If every person at your place of work cared only for him- or herself, it would be impossible to get anything done. You couldn't count on your peers to help you meet tight deadlines or correct mistakes. You couldn't count on your boss to give you credit when you've done a good job. You couldn't trust your co-workers to put the interests of the company before their own. The atmosphere in the workplace would be full of distrust, competitiveness, and selfishness.

Why would you want to work hard if no one were willing to help you, if your boss would not give you credit, or if no one cared about you or the job? The truth is you would learn not to care, too. This is why successful businesspeople encourage their employees to work as part of a team.

What Is a Team?

A team is a group of people working together toward a common goal. In business, that goal is to produce high-quality goods and services that will satisfy the customer. Teamwork, however, is an idea that has been around much longer than modern business.

Sharing a Common Goal

For the earliest civilizations, the shared goal was to survive. The survival of a group depended on teamwork. Each group member played a specific role in gathering food, building shelter, and defending the group against the enemy. If one person were lost, the survival of the whole group was at stake. Throughout history, teamwork played a major role in helping civilizations to progress. Groups formed societies; societies formed nations; and nations developed systems of government. Our democratic society is an example of what teamwork can accomplish. Our society is built on a system of checks and balances in which the three branches of government work together

Get Savvy: Myth versus Fact

Myth: You don't get individual recognition when you work in a team.

Fact: There's more opportunity for recognition because more people see your work.

to run the country. Each branch of government also is organized around teams. In each department, bureau, office, section, or group, people work together to make sure our system operates effectively. Teamwork has come to represent our nation's identity. In every part of our society, you'll find people working in teams.

What's the Point of Teamwork?

Productivity and *efficiency* are two very important words in business; they are a big part of why teamwork is valuable.

Productivity

Productivity is the amount of work completed in a given period of time. It's a measure of how much work a person or group can accomplish in a certain amount of time. If you have high productivity, you can get a lot done. Usually, a person has high productivity because he or she works efficiently.

productivity amount of work completed per period of time

Efficiency

Efficiency is doing a job without wasting time, materials, or energy. It makes sense that if someone can complete a task without wasting time, that person will be able to do more in less time and will have higher productivity. The following examples compare high efficiency and productivity to low efficiency and productivity.

efficiency the ability to complete a task without wasting time, materials, or energy

How Do You Achieve High Productivity?

One of your good friends is a DJ who has a gig coming up at a local club. He asks two of his friends, Maria and Craig, to help him advertise by posting flyers. He gives each of them 100 flyers to hang in shops and restaurants.

Maria's Approach

Before Maria leaves with her flyers, she looks up the names and locations of businesses where students hang out. She calls ahead to those places to make sure she has permission to post her flyers. She makes a list so she can save time by skipping businesses that don't allow flyers.

When Maria arrives at each location, she immediately posts her flyers with the tape and thumbtacks she brought with her. She hands out the rest to people eating lunch and shopping.

It took Maria 15 minutes to make her calls, plus an hour to get to town and post all her flyers. She has time left over to relax and have a cup of coffee.

Craig's Approach

Craig heads straight to his favorite coffee shop on the other side of town. He doesn't think about how long it will take to get there or if there are other businesses nearby.

Craig still has to ask for permission to post his flyers. The server tells Craig that he has to ask the manager, who won't be in for another 15 minutes.

Craig realizes he didn't bring any tape, and the server only has heavy-duty tape. Craig rips three flyers trying to use it to tack them up.

Craig still has to travel back across town to find more shops to cover. After an hour, he has posted only 25 of his 100 flyers. He gives up and goes home.

As these examples illustrate, some methods get better results than others. Working efficiently is one way to increase your productivity. Which friend accomplished the most in the same amount of time? Look at Figure 2.1 and compare.

Figure 2.1 *You Be the Judge*

And the winning approach for productivity is...

Maria's Approach	Craig's Approach
Thoughtful preparation	No preparation
Targeted nearby businesses	Targeted only one far-off business
Called ahead to store managers	Didn't call ahead
Brought along necessary tools	Had to borrow inappropriate tools
Posted 100 flyers	Posted 25 flyers

Thinking Critically There are differences between Maria's approach and Craig's approach. *How could the situation have been improved if Maria and Craig had worked as a team?*

New Attitudes / New Opportunities

Meet Alita Mitchell. Alita is a 30-year-old, single woman studying criminal justice at Myers College in Cleveland, Ohio. She plans to graduate soon. Her professional background consists mainly of office work as an accounting assistant. Here's what she had to say on . . . .

Going Back to School "School was something that I always wanted to do, but the timing wasn't right for me when I was younger. I know that to make it in today's society, you need some kind of educational background. So getting a degree became a goal."

Her Career Goals and What She Wants to Do with Her Degree "If I make it to law school, I want to be a family law attorney or do some type of counseling. I'd really like to help people who've been caught up in the system."

The Benefits and Drawbacks of Working in a Team "The overall thing about teamwork is that we're all working for the same company. If you realize that we all have the same goal, you can pull together as a team if a department needs help. While working, you will meet all types of people. A drawback of teamwork is that sometimes, even though you may be the type of person that is able to communicate with others, you have to work with people who aren't so able to communicate with you."

Learning Things the Hard Way "Sometimes you work with people who don't really give good instructions. You get an assignment and you're thinking, 'OK, how am I going to figure this out?' Because I don't want to mess up anything, I've learned it's OK to go back and ask questions. That's part of teamwork."

Working Smart

Even though Maria accomplished her personal goal, and her productivity was high, she and Craig together still only distributed 125 of the 200 flyers set as their team goal. If they had worked together to increase efficiency, they could have increased the productivity of the team. What could they do differently?

- Each teammate could call a certain number of businesses in advance. Or one could look up store numbers, while the other starts calling.
- When working on site, one teammate could post flyers while the other hands them out to customers.
- While one drives to the site, the others could prepare the flyers for posting by putting the tape in place.

Accomplishing a team goal by working more closely together would have been fun as well as rewarding. Maria and Craig would have had a good time and impressed their DJ friend—he might even have given them free tickets to the show as thanks for their good work.

> The keynote of progress, we should remember, is not merely doing away with what is bad; it is replacing the best with something better.
>
> *Edward A. Filene*
> *American Merchant, Founder of Filene's Department Stores*

What Are the Perks of Teamwork?

As our example demonstrates, working in a team has several benefits. For one, you may have more fun when you work with other people. If you enjoy what you do, you'll keep doing it, unlike Craig who gave up when things weren't going his way.

Collaboration

Collaboration is another word for working together. You hear this word used a lot to describe musicians who collaborate on CDs, or directors and writers who collaborate on films. These artists combine their talents and creativity to come up with better ideas or products, which is another perk of teamwork. Collaboration is at the heart of teamwork. Teamwork is all about succeeding by taking advantage of every team member's individual talents. A famous guitarist might collaborate with an equally talented vocalist. Both artists combine their individual talents to make some seriously good music. More importantly, they share the credit. They both know that they couldn't have made the music without the other.

Motivation

When you collaborate as part of an effective team, you are motivated because you enjoy what you do, and because you know that other people count on you to do a good job. In other words, teamwork keeps you motivated. *Motivation* is a word that is used a lot these days. You hear about motivational speakers and motivational books. Actors ask directors, "What's my motivation?" From time to time you may even tell yourself, "Get motivated! Turn off the TV! Get off the couch and do some work!" **Motivation** is the impulse or drive that causes us to act. Your motivation to get off the couch might be the paycheck you'll receive at the end of the week. Your motivation for going to class is probably the desire to get an education so you can live a better, more fulfilled life; or your motivation to post 200 flyers as efficiently as possible might be to gain the satisfaction of working together with others toward a common goal.

Collaboration, Motivation, and Trust

Collaboration combined with motivation will lead to trust. You have read that a team consists of a group of people working toward a common goal. Whether that goal is to post 200 flyers or to provide friendly customer service, everyone on the team wants to meet it. This means you and your teammates all have the same interest. Your personal success depends on the success of the team. It's the same for every one of your teammates; you each have a stake in the success of the team. This common interest takes competition and selfishness out of the picture. Instead of racing to impress the boss or stand out among peers, teammates work together to meet their goals. No one wastes energy on nonproductive activity. Everyone uses that energy to solve problems, meet deadlines, satisfy customers-or post flyers, as the case may be. When co-workers aren't competing with each other, they are free to trust one another.

Responsibility With trust comes responsibility. **Responsibility** means accountability. Your teammates depend on you to do a good job. In fact, they trust that you won't let them down by procrastinating, being lazy, taking long lunches, or doing poor work. When people you trust depend on you, you will be motivated to do your best. They will do the same for you and, together, you will encourage each other to succeed. If any member or part of the team fails, the team as a whole fails. If the team succeeds, the success belongs to everyone.

Once it is established that everyone on a team is working together, it is easier to share ideas. Remember, you all have a common interest. There is no way one person can take all the credit for the work of a team. It would be as if the guitarist took credit for the vocals on that CD. When you can trust that everyone has the same interests, then you will start collaborating.

Dr. Joe Pace
TAKING
RESPONSIBILITY

"Responsibility teaches us to take control over ourselves and our futures: 'If it's to be, it's up to me.'"

Advantages   Collaboration and trust within a team produces

- Better ideas and products.
- More efficient use of time.
- Happier, more productive workers.
- Fewer opportunities for errors.

QUICK RECAP 2.1

THE IMPORTANCE OF TEAMWORK

Now you should have a better idea of the benefits and importance of teamwork. Here is a quick summary of why teamwork is important.

- Teams work more efficiently and have higher productivity than individuals.
- Team members are motivated by a common goal and shared interests.
- When you work in a team, you collaborate because you know that you share goals with your teammates.
- When you work in a team, you produce good work because your teammates help you check for quality.
- When you trust and respect your teammates, you enjoy working together and, therefore, enjoy what you do.

CHECK YOURSELF

1. Name one thing that all members of a team share.
2. List three advantages of teamwork.

Check your answers online at **www.mhhe.com/pace.**

BUSINESS VOCABULARY

collaboration   the act of working together, combining talents and skills
efficiency   the ability to complete a task without wasting time, materials, or energy
motivation   the reason or drive to do something
productivity   amount of work completed per period of time
responsibility   an obligation or task for which you are accountable

Where Teamwork Starts

In the last section, you learned about the importance of teamwork in a business setting. You learned that collaboration is the first step in developing an effective team. You also learned that trust and respect among teammates result from collaborating effectively.

Where Do I Start? This section discusses some specific ways you can earn the respect of your teammates and show your respect for them. By learning and practicing individual teamwork skills, you can make collaborating with your teammates easier. Teamwork skills include approaching others with respect; listening carefully; communicating clearly; being flexible; and exhibiting tolerance and understanding. All of these skills begin with showing respect for each team member's ideas, talents, personality, beliefs, and approach to work and life. When all members of a team use their individual teamwork skills, collaboration can happen, and teamwork starts.

Reading and Study Tip

Text Organization
Paragraphs can be organized in different ways. Some start with a statement and follow with examples. As you read this section, look for statements followed by examples.

Approaching Others with Respect

Take a minute to think about how you interact with people. Do you like to hang out with a crowd, play team sports, or act in plays? Maybe you prefer solitary walks in the park, reading a good book, or watching TV. More importantly, do you get along well with people when you are in a group?

Know Yourself

Thinking about how you interact with people on a day-to-day basis will give you a good idea of how effective you will be as a working team member. Whether you are outgoing or shy, the way you treat people when you interact with them is what's important when working on a team.

Pace Points

Walk a Mile in My Shoes
Next time you disagree with someone, take a minute to consider that person's point of view before you make any judgments.

Treat Teammates with Regard

A person who is outgoing and popular isn't automatically better at teamwork than someone who prefers reading quietly in the library. The athlete who hogs the ball or blames everyone else when the team loses, but takes all the credit when they win, isn't a good team player. No one enjoys playing with a person like that. On the other hand, the reader who always helps new students find books in the library and listens to other people's opinions about literature would make a great teammate. This person takes the time to help others, listen to their ideas, and be respectful of their opinions.

Listening Carefully

Truly listening to someone is an art form that requires respect. Most of us think we are good at it, but we may not realize that there's a lot we miss when we have a conversation. Too often, we may not listen carefully because we're distracted, or we're trying to do too many things at once. Listening intently, in spite of distractions, is especially important in a teamwork situation. The exchange of ideas is one of the main reasons people work in teams. When team members don't pay attention to each other's ideas, the team can lose its creative edge.

Know When to Listen

Sometimes, we don't listen because we assume we know what someone is going to say before he or she says it. Did you ever have a hard time listening to a teacher who told the same stories over and over? Sometimes it's hard not to "tune out" someone like that. When we assume we know what someone will say, we often stop listening. If we stop listening, we may miss important information, instructions, and ideas.

When we don't listen carefully, we also communicate a lack of respect to the person who's talking. Have you ever tried to explain something or confide in a friend when you knew that friend was not paying attention? It might have felt frustrating or hurt your feelings. When we listen carefully to someone, we show that we value what he or she has to say. Listening intently is a sign of respect.

Listen and Remember

If you are paying attention to someone, you are listening *and* remembering. Do you recall the last time you were having a chat with a classmate? Do you remember what it was about? Where did he go last Friday night? What's his girlfriend's name? Does he even have a girlfriend? We tend to ignore or forget information that we don't think is important or interesting. As the saying goes: "In one ear and out the other." You can bet, however, that your classmate thinks his girlfriend's name is pretty important. By making an effort to listen and remember details, you show your respect. This same behavior helps you work effectively in a team.

Communicating Clearly

Being a good talker sometimes means that you can speak comfortably in class, or make conversation easily when you meet new people. In terms of teamwork, however, a good talker is one who is understood. Communication is vital to teamwork, and misunderstood communication can be a big obstacle to collaborating effectively. If your teammates get the wrong idea from something you've said, or they simply don't understand what you mean, work can come to a standstill.

> " *It is better to understand a little than to misunderstand a lot.* "
>
> **Anatole France**
> *French Writer and Critic*

Choose Your Words Carefully

We all know how easy it is to get into the habit of using words and phrases such as *like, stuff,* and **you know what I mean.** Well, the truth is, people usually don't know what you mean. You can't assume that people understand what you are trying to say if you aren't clear and specific.

To be understood,

- Speak clearly and concisely.
- Avoid slang or abbreviations.
- Use appropriate language.
- Avoid street or offensive language.

Retail Etiquette

Your Challenge

You work as a sales representative for a well-known store. One of your co-workers constantly uses street language around the workplace. You have tolerated it when you are working alone together, but now you notice that she is beginning to swear in meetings and in front of customers. What do you do?

The Possibilities

A. Immediately file a complaint with the human resources department and your boss.

B. Ignore the behavior and assume that it's her problem if she gets in trouble.

C. Discuss the problem casually with the person and ask her to stop.

D. Accept swearing as normal in that office and join in.

Your Solution

Choose the solution that you think will be most effective and write a few sentences explaining your opinion on a separate sheet of paper. Then check your answer with the answer on our Web site: www.mhhe.com/pace.

Express Your Thoughts Completely

Another way to avoid miscommunication is to give your listeners background information. If you watch soap operas, you may have noticed that the characters have the most unnatural conversations. They say things like, "Blake, do you remember the night two years ago when my mother came back from the dead at Robin's Christmas party?" "Yes, Miriam, the party where you wore the blue dress, the one your first husband Storm—who was really his twin brother Erik—gave you."

This dialogue is packed with seemingly unimportant and expositional information. Why? So that TV viewers who don't watch every day will know what's been happening. If Miriam had said, "Blake, do you remember when my mother came back from the dead?" And Blake responded, "Yes, you were wearing the blue dress," the scene would have no meaning at all.

You'll certainly have more credible conversations than Blake and Miriam, but you can learn from their example. Make it a habit to assume that your listeners do not have any background information. Complete information is the best way to prevent confusion and misunderstanding

Be Polite

As well as being clear, concise, and professional, it is important to be respectful in the way we communicate with others. The words *please* and *thank you* are common in any language, but as you meet people from different backgrounds, you'll realize people communicate in different ways. What sounds curt and rude to you may appear direct and honest to a teammate. The same goes for what *we* say. What we find inoffensive or harmless may sound rude to a listener. It helps to use common sense and watch reactions. If you're not sure if something is offensive, ask politely. You show a great deal of respect when you let someone know that you do not want to offend him or her.

Learn How to Disagree   At times we all disagree with someone. It is important to learn to express that disagreement constructively. Here are some tips for constructive disagreement:

- State your case politely. Remember, you want the other person or persons to listen to your opinion.
- Keep the discussion impersonal. Keep your issue about a decision or an act, not a person.
- Show respect for the other person's argument. If you deliver your point of view with respect, it is much more likely to be treated with respect.

Being Flexible

Nothing in this world stays the same. Conditions are always changing, and it is our ability to adapt that allows us to survive. To **adapt** means to change to fit something. A flexible person is one who can change to suit new circumstances. When a workplace situation changes, all employees have to be ready to adapt to it. People who cannot adapt to change in the workplace are unhappy, unproductive, and often replaced.

Learn to Adapt

Can you imagine office life before the invention of the fax machine, photocopier, and computer? Businesses have had to adapt to new ways of doing things in order to be competitive. No company operates the same way it did 20 years ago. These days, a company without a Web site will most likely lose business to a competitor who has an online presence.

Similarly, if you have a difficult time working with new people, ideas, and systems, you will have a difficult time contributing as a team member. Developing the ability to adapt to new ideas and technologies will help you be an effective team member.

Challenge Yourself   The fact that you are reading this book shows that you are flexible and motivated to learn new ideas and systems. However, it's very easy to begin to make changes and then stop. Sometimes we think we've made enough changes. Sometimes we're a little nervous about what change might bring. Sometimes we think we've adapted to change, when others might not agree. To keep up with change, try challenging yourself.

One of the benefits of teamwork is that you have an opportunity take on different responsibilities within a team. For example, suppose you work on the company newsletter committee. Your job is to get photos from each department. You are really good at this job, but you also like working with numbers. Challenge yourself. Ask your team to let you help with budgets and schedules. This way you get to try something new and still have your teammates to help you while you learn. Next time the person in charge of budgets needs a hand, he or she will come to you knowing that you are flexible and can do the job.

Exhibiting Tolerance and Understanding

A team cannot work effectively if teammates don't show tolerance and understanding of each other's differences. **Tolerance** is the willingness to accept things that are different. You have probably heard the term *diversity* used around your campus or workplace. **Diversity** means variety, assortment, or mixture. Figure 2.2 lists teamwork skills that you can practice by applying tolerance and an understanding of diversity.

> *Maturity involves being honest and true to oneself . . . . assuming responsibility for one's decisions, having healthy relationships with others and developing one's own true gifts.*
>
> *Mary Pipher*
> *Psychologist*

adapt to change to suit new circumstances

> *No human trait deserves less tolerance in everyday life and gets less, than intolerance.*
>
> *Giacomo Leopardi*
> *Italian Poet and Philosopher*

tolerance respect of the beliefs and practices of others

diversity variety of different people, ideas, or things

Figure 2.2 *Teamwork Skills*

Learn To...	By...	And You'll...
Approach others with respect	Knowing yourself and treating teammates fairly	Contribute as an effective team player.
Listen carefully	Listening and remembering	Show others that you respect and value their opinions.
Communicate clearly	Choosing your words carefully, expressing your thoughts completely, being polite, and learning how to disagree	Avoid miscommunication.
Be flexible	Learning to adapt and challenging yourself	Respond positively to new situations.
Exhibit understanding and tolerance	Respecting diversity and earning the trust of all	Realize that people aren't that different after all.

Thinking Critically Effective teamwork skills are based on tolerance, respect of diversity, and trust. *What other positive results will come from practicing good teamwork skills?*

Respect Diversity

A diverse group is one that includes people from different ethnic, racial, economic, and religious backgrounds. In today's world, diversity makes you and your teammates unique. For example, people from different backgrounds might have different reactions to the same situation. To make teamwork effective, let your teammates tackle a problem in their own ways. Keep an open mind. Reserve your judgment until you know all the facts. You'll probably realize that people are not that different after all.

Earn the Trust of All

Tolerance and understanding of diversity will help you interact with others in a positive way. However, you may not always approve of your teammates' lifestyle choices or points of view. That's your right. However, realize that it is also their right to live as they have chosen. Reserve judgment and keep your opinions about lifestyles to yourself. Demonstrate an understanding of the basic rights we all share by accommodating teammates who practice religious customs or have special needs that are different from yours.

The Power of One

So now you know what you can do to build trust and respect among your teammates—to be an effective team player. By using these skills, you will be ahead of the game when you sit down for your first team meeting. Now it's time to ask the question: "What happens if I'm teamed up with people who haven't practiced these skills?"

Be a Role Model

The answer is simple. By practicing your teamwork skills, you can set the example for the team. If every team member practices the same good teamwork behavior demonstrated by you, that behavior will become the standard for the team. Teamwork, like any good relationship, is about give and take and meeting each other half way. When all the team members make an effort to respect and trust each other, then they can all share credit for the team's successes.

QUICK RECAP 2.2

WHERE TEAMWORK STARTS

- Whether you are outgoing or shy, the way you treat people when you interact with them is what's important when working on a team.
- The exchange of ideas is one of the main reasons why people work in teams.
- Showing others that you respect their points of view is the best way to deal with a difference of opinion.
- A flexible person is one who can change to suit new circumstances. When a workplace situation changes, you have to be ready to adapt to it.
- Tolerance and understanding will help you interact with others in a positive way and earn their trust.

CHECK YOURSELF

1. What is one reason it is important to listen effectively?
2. How can you set the standard of behavior for your team?

Check your answers online at **www.mhhe.com/pace.** *Pace* ONLINE

BUSINESS VOCABULARY

adapt   to change to suit new circumstances
diversity   variety of different people, ideas, or things
tolerance   respect of the beliefs and practices of others

Organizing a Team

Now that you know how to be a good team member, you're ready to learn how a good team stays organized. Knowing how to organize can make you an even more valuable team member—one who is recognized by others as having leadership potential.

Sorting To organize is to sort things according to **attributes** or qualities. In this section we are going to talk about three aspects of team organization: developing a personal approach to organization; organizing team goals and tracking progress; and organizing team members to get the job done.

attributes characteristics that describe a person or thing

categorizing grouping things according to their common attributes

What Is Organizing?

You probably started formal learning of organizational skills in kindergarten. The teacher handed you some different colored blocks, and you made a pile of red ones and another pile of green ones. Later you learned how to sort numbers into groups, such as evens and odds, multiples of three, factors of 16, and so on. You were beginning to acquire your organizational skills.

As you become more skilled at organization, you will automatically see how things are related to each other, and you will be able to group them based on common factors.

Categorizing

Organizing things into groups based on common factors is called **categorizing.** The Yellow Pages phone book is a great example of how categorizing information makes it handy and usable. Each listing is grouped by service and then alphabetized. To find Ray's Pizza, you look up *Restaurants,* then *Pizza,* and then you look under the Rs to find the number for Ray's. Each category is a subsection of the one before it.

In a similar way, you can organize a team of people into subsections or groups based on skills or talents. You also can organize goals into the specific steps needed to achieve them.

Developing a Personal Approach to Organization

How you organize yourself reflects your personal approach to work and life. A casual system of organization may work for a while, but the demands of a full schedule and other people depending on you eventually will force you to get organized in a more formal way.

Organize for Efficiency

Having an organized approach allows us to work more efficiently. Remember, efficiency means not wasting time, materials, or energy. Instead of wasting time searching for information on a messy desk, the organized person just turns to the appropriate page in his or her planner. When we are not wasting time, we are more efficient.

You may already understand the importance of being organized. For example, when you take notes in class, do you

- Write down the date at the top of the page?
- Note the topic of the day's lecture?
- Underline important ideas or star key sentences?
- Jot down the page numbers of the corresponding chapter in your textbook?
- Label your notes and put them together in a class binder or folder?

If you do these things, you will be organized when it's time for your final exam. You'll know exactly where to find a semester's worth of class notes.

These are good habits to develop—exactly the kinds of habits you need when you enter the working world. Developing these skills now means that when you get a job, you'll be reliable and responsible, and you'll most likely get your work done right the first time.

Organize for Teamwork

When several people work together as a team, being organized is even more essential to getting things done properly. As part of a team, you'll probably share files, books, materials, and information with your teammates. You'll need to know where everything is and how to find it. More importantly, you'll need to be able to tell other people how they can access important information about projects you've been working on.

In a team environment, assignments may overlap. Work is divided, and more than one person is assigned to the same aspects of a project. Part of working together is sharing each other's resources and skills. You may be responsible for collecting information that one of your teammates needs in order to complete his or her particular assignment. If you are not organized, you won't be a very productive team member. With good organizational habits, you will be able to make a positive contribution to your team.

Organizing Team Goals and Tracking Progress

Long-term goals are achieved by working hard at a series of less-ambitious short-term goals that will add up to success. **Short-term goals** are the immediate targets that your team aims for to succeed.

The ultimate goal of a baseball team at the beginning of the season is to win the World Series. Let's look at some short-term goals in outline form:

- Win the most games of the season.
  - Win the first game.
  - Get players on base.
  - Prevent opponent from scoring.

In a business environment, every short-term goal is designed to get the business one step closer to the long-term goal of success.

Pace Points

Go the Extra Mile
Be careful doing your work. It's more work to go back and correct an ignored or overlooked mistake than it is to do it right the first time.

long-term goal an ultimate goal of any effort

short-term goal an attainable objective that helps achieve a greater goal

Tips From a Mentor

Getting Organized

Top ten ways you can stay organized:

- **Use organizational tools.** Get a personal planner and use it. Keep all your addresses, important information, and schedules together. Use briefcases, binders, divided file folders, divided notebooks, or anything else that will help you stay organized.

- **Make daily lists** of what you want to accomplish at work or school. As you complete a job, cross it off the list. This reminds you how much you accomplished that day.

- **Keep a pen and pad with you at all times** to take notes in meetings, record conversations, and jot down ideas as they come. Use this information in your "To Do" list.

- **Keep project files separate, organized, and available.** Always file materials neatly and accurately so you can easily find any details you need.

- **Keep a profile of the people with whom you do business.** This should include their business cards, their résumés, any correspondence you've had, and any information you can find about them or their work from a company Web site. This way, you will know with whom you are dealing and will be able to have intelligent conversations about the person's work.

- **Keep your workspace tidy.** Everything in your office or study room should have its place. Have an organizational system and stick to it.

- **Label everything.** This includes faxes, correspondence, e-mail, files, folders, receipts, computer files, and disks. Always assign a title, list the date, and note your name and contact information.

- **Use shared drives or office networks.** Determine a location and a labeling system for electronic files. Make sure everyone sticks to this system so you will all be able to locate projects.

- **Back up important files and correspondence** by keeping copies available, especially when sending out information. Never send an original document unless required. Back up any information on your hard drive onto disks that are regularly updated.

- **Don't throw anything away until you are sure you don't need it.** This includes research, project information, ideas, and contact information. Regularly update your files; if space allows, hang on to information. You never know when it will come in handy.

Action Steps

action steps the specific tasks your team needs to complete in order to achieve a goal

Short-term goals can be broken down into even smaller action steps. **Action steps** are the specific tasks your team needs to complete in order to achieve a goal. They help you get started. The first man at bat gets a base hit; the second gets a double; the third walks; and the fourth cleans up with a grand-slam home run. Score: four to zip.

Action steps can be the kinds of tasks you would find on a "To Do" list at work or at home. For example, if you are throwing a dinner party, your action steps might include the following:

- Send out invitations.
- Plan the menu.

- Clean the house.
- Buy ingredients.
- Set the table.
- Prepare the appetizers, main dish, and dessert.

Outlining action steps can help you grapple with a broad and sometimes overwhelming goal by breaking it down into a sequence of smaller, more achievable jobs. In the case of the baseball team faced with a tough opponent, the action steps might be to stack the line-up with strong hitters and take advantage of the opposing pitcher's fastball. By outlining action steps, you can come up with a plan or strategy for reaching your short-term goal. Once you've reached that short-term goal, you are one step closer to success.

Planning and Prioritizing Action Steps

To outline a series of action steps designed to meet a short-term goal, consider the questions "How to . . . ." and "What is needed to . . . ."

Find a Toehold Approach the "How to . . . ." question the way a mountain climber approaches a steep cliff. First find a toehold. Find a small step you can take to get you moving. For example, the short-term goal assigned to your team at your new job is to find 20 new clients for your department. The assignment may seem overwhelming, like looking up the face of a mountain. As part of your strategy, you look for a toehold. In other words, find a starting place and take that first step. After the first step, it becomes easier to make a plan.

To meet your goal of getting 20 clients, make a plan with these steps:

- **Step 1** Instead of looking for 20 clients at once, have teammates each take a share of new clients.
- **Step 2** Call clients from your last job for referrals. Ask all team members to use their networks for referrals.
- **Step 3** Contact referrals. Use those contacts for more referrals.

Think about Resources Approach the "What is needed to . . . ." question by thinking about the resources you and your team will need to put your plan into action. Look again at the action steps listed for putting on a dinner party. See how each step includes the answer to the questions of "How to put on a dinner party" and "What is needed to put on a dinner party?"

How To...	What Is Needed To...
Send out invitations	Invitations, envelopes, stamps
Plan the menu	Cookbooks, favorite recipes
Clean the house	Cleaning supplies
Buy ingredients	Menu plan, shopping list
Set the table	Dinnerware, silverware, napkins,
Prepare the appetizers, main dish, and dessert	Ingredients

Plan B

Don't be afraid to deviate from your planned action steps. If a good idea comes up, use it, even if it wasn't in the plan. And if your plan isn't working, scrap it! Don't be afraid to start over.

Figure 2.3 *Planning*

Thinking Critically You can reach your goals with an organized plan. *How would you prioritize the action steps listed here?*

prioritize to order ideas, items, or tasks according to importance

Prioritize To **prioritize** is to order items, ideas, or procedures according to importance. Start with the most important. Your first and most important action steps are the ones that have to be done before you can move on to the next step. Once you have a step-by-step outline of how to achieve your goal, you can get to work. Don't forget that achieving a goal, like winning a baseball game, is a step-by-step process. Each move builds on the one before it. Having an organized plan of action steps, such as the "To Do" list in Figure 2.3, will help you reach your goal more efficiently.

Organizing Team Members to Get the Job Done

- Teams can be organized into different subsections or groups, each with a different function.
- Each group takes on a specific role that is defined by a set of responsibilities.
- Different groups can be working on different aspects of a project at the same time.
- When different parts of a team work independently, someone must keep track of
  - What needs to be done.
  - Who's doing what.
  - When tasks need to be completed.

Figure 2.4 *Organization by Function*

Personal Planner Organization	Team Organization
Project section	Project manager
Calendar	Schedule manager
Notes and information section	Information manager
Expenses and finance section	Bookkeeper or financial tracker
Address and phone book	Communications manager

Thinking Critically Different groups can work together to get a job done. *Have you been part of a team in which the members were organized according to function?*

Think about how you organize your school notes or your personal planner. In your personal planner, the categories reflect specific functions. You may have a project section, calendar section, information section, expenses and finance section, and your address book.

Compare team organization to organizing a personal planner in Figure 2.4.

Project Managers

The project page of your planner is where you can outline projects you are working on. You can *jot down ideas, list short-term goals,* and *outline* and *prioritize your action steps.*

When tackling a team assignment, the team gets started by planning action steps. This need creates role number one within the team: project management. Project managers are the people responsible for defining the action steps. The project manager can flesh out each action step to identify

- How to . . . .
- What is needed to . . . .

Also, if something comes up that isn't in the original plan, a project manager can define and assign new action steps.

Project managers are still team members, but they usually have had more experience with the various functions of a team than others. They keep an eye on the big picture: the team's long-term goal. They track the team's progress to make sure the team is heading in the right direction and not getting sidetracked.

Schedule Managers

You use the calendar pages of your planner to

- Plan and record your schedule.
- Keep track of deadlines.
- Schedule appointments.

It is an essential tool to help you manage your time and make the most out of your day.

Having a team member perform a scheduling function for the team will help ensure that goals are met on time. The schedule manager

- Knows the availability and time commitments of each team member.
- Sets general deadlines.
- Keeps each group informed of their particular deadlines for action steps.
- Keeps an up-to-date schedule of team meetings and appointments.

Information Managers

The information section of a planner is a space set aside for you to keep important notes, lists, and reminders. A good team should have people who function in the same way. Information managers keep track of the information the team needs to complete their action steps. They are in charge of researching each project so that their teammates can make the right decisions when working with customers and vendors. They also are in charge of organizing, updating, and maintaining information files and databases. They keep the team aware of changes in information or details. The person performing this function needs to be especially organized.

Financial Tracking

The financial section of a planner is a place where you can *record what you've spent, balance your accounts,* and *outline a budget.* The corresponding section of a team is the group or person responsible for accounting. These people *outline the team's budget for a project.* They decide how much money is needed to meet the team's goals and they *allocate the necessary amounts* to each group. They also *keep track of group expenses* and *make sure that the team is on budget.* They deal with all the financial aspects of achieving a team's action steps and short-term goals. They help the team run efficiently by paying attention to how much money the team spends and making sure that money is not wasted.

Communications

Most planners have a section for addresses, e-mail addresses, and phone numbers. This section is different from the information section because its main purpose is to make communicating with people easier. On a team, the people in charge of communications perform this function. They make sure that everyone keeps each other posted on their progress. They keep the address and phone book for the team. These people know *how and where to contact team members* to *arrange meetings* and *distribute minutes and memos.* They also keep track of all the important contacts outside of the company who need to be informed of the team's accomplishments. They may even communicate with the public, the press, and clients. Most importantly, they keep communication between different branches of a team flowing, so everyone is on the same page.

Assigning Functions

aptitudes natural abilities, tendencies, or talents

Assigning functions to team members is an important role. Everyone possesses certain skills and aptitudes. **Aptitudes** are the abilities that allow a person to be good at a particular job. Some of us have an aptitude for numbers. For others, it's a flare for writing. Your aptitude for a job should determine your role on a team. If you are good with numbers, you should probably work with the financial tracking group instead of the communications group. All team members should enjoy what they do. Usually, if you do something that you are good at, you will enjoy your work.

Team projects are a great opportunity to try a job for which you have an aptitude but not much experience. As you build experience in different areas, you can develop a sense of how a team functions. This knowledge prepares you to move into a leadership position where you can help set short-term goals and plan action steps.

Although functions and roles may vary from team to team, team functions are vital to the operation of a team as a whole. As you become more familiar with different functions, you will be able to see how they all fit together. You may have noticed that having an organized approach is all about efficiency. When everyone on a team is organized, all the functions of a team can operate together. Now the team can make real progress toward achieving its goals.

QUICK RECAP 2.3

ORGANIZING A TEAM

- Organizing things into groups based on common factors is called *categorizing.*
- A casual system of organization may work for a while, but the demands of a full schedule will eventually force you to get organized in a more formal way.
- To help demonstrate how teams can be organized into groups, think of each subsection or group in a team as a section of a personal planner. Each group of team members performs a different set of functions.
- Try to be assigned to a team function for which you have an aptitude.

CHECK YOURSELF

1. List one reason why it is important to have an organized approach to teamwork.
2. What are the different functions of an organized team?

Check your answers online at **www.mhhe.com/pace.** *Pace* ONLINE

BUSINESS VOCABULARY

action steps   the specific tasks your team needs to complete in order to achieve a goal
aptitude   natural abilities, tendencies, or talents
attributes   characteristics that describe a person or thing
categorizing   grouping things according to their common attributes
long-term goal   an ultimate goal of any effort
prioritize   to order ideas, items, or tasks according to importance
short-term goal   an attainable objective that helps achieve a greater goal

Negotiating and Resolving Conflict

When people get together and combine their talents as a team, they have the potential to get a lot done. They also have the potential for disagreement, or **conflict.** The success of a team depends on its members being able to work together in a positive way. That's why you learn individual teamwork skills. You only have to look at history, though, to realize that, every now and again, people or groups of people just don't get along. The effects of conflict among team members are the biggest obstacles to building a successful team.

Conflict Creates Obstacles   There are many different types of people in this world, and not everyone will understand the value of trust and respect the same way you do. It is likely that, at some point in your career, you will work with a person who has a negative attitude. By practicing your individual teamwork skills, you can be sure that you'll never be one of these negative people. In the meantime, you still have to work together. This section will teach you how to handle difficult situations. You will learn how to recognize, resolve, and prevent conflict among team members.

conflict a sharp disagreement in interests or ideas

Imbalance in the Team

There are many causes of conflict among team members. Sometimes two people have personality differences and just don't like each other. If you get off to a bad start with someone, a bad first impression can be hard to shake. There isn't a lot you can do to make people like each other. Personal disputes or dislikes should not affect the team if everyone uses individual teamwork skills. When all are working for the success of the team in a respectful and professional way, personal differences don't get in the way of work.

Pulling Your Own Weight

On a successful team, the workload is divided into tasks and distributed equally among team members. You may have heard the expressions "Around here, everyone pulls his or her weight" or "There are no free rides." This means that everyone is expected to do the same amount of work. That's how a good team should function. When responsibilities are divided evenly, teammates depend on each other to complete a team project, and responsibility for the team's performance is shared.

Picking up the Slack   When conflict between individuals or groups keeps people from doing their jobs, the balance of the whole team is upset. The team stops being productive. Sometimes teammates have additional work because they pick up the slack for those in conflict.

When people don't "pull their weight," resentment and conflict can be the result. Everyone loses sight of the team's goals, and a team can break down. It's like throwing a wrench into the works of a well-oiled machine. If one part doesn't work, the whole machine fails.

For example, a conflict between teammates who share responsibility for communications can halt the progress of the entire team. The squabbling co-workers responsible for scheduling aren't talking to one another. So, they each set the time for a meeting on different dates. Half the team shows up one day and half the other. In this case, negative behavior wastes the time of the entire team. This type of individual conflict can start a cycle leading to blame, resentment, and even bigger conflicts.

Recognizing the Causes of Conflict

Being able to recognize the causes of conflict is an important part of preventing conflict. At the heart of most conflict is lack of respect. Lack of respect usually develops when someone exhibits a negative or unprofessional attitude. All of us want to be taken seriously and treated with respect. Teammates can politely and constructively disagree; it happens all the time. Often, a feeling of lack of respect can turn a small disagreement into a bigger conflict. These conflicts involve a negative or unprofessional attitude on the part of two or more teammates.

Complaining

A complainer is a person who is critical of everything. A complainer shows a negative attitude by picking things apart instead of offering helpful solutions to problems. People usually don't have much patience for complaining. If you find yourself complaining about a problem, do something about it. Complaining is not efficient. While you waste time complaining, you could be fixing the problem. This behavior eventually will cause conflict among teammates. Individual teamwork skills—listening effectively, communicating effectively, being flexible, and showing tolerance and respect—should be the standard of behavior for every member of a team. Anyone who complains—constantly is not listening or communicating clearly.

> *It is much easier to be critical than to be correct.*
>
> *Benjamin Disraeli*
> *19th-Century British Prime Minister*

Being Lazy

Another big cause of conflict is plain old laziness. Some people don't take pride in their work. This affects the whole team. Lazy people do the least work possible and usually can't meet difficult deadlines. Someone will have to pick up the slack, and that someone will not be happy about it. Everyone on a team has work to do, and nobody wants to spend time correcting mistakes or finishing other people's projects. Laziness is unprofessional and will most certainly be a cause of stress within the group. Laziness is a very real cause of conflict.

Being Judgmental

Having a negative attitude also can mean that you always assume the worst about people or situations. There are plenty of gossips, game players, back stabbers, and office politicians in the business world. These people tend to focus only on what's good for them. They create conflict by focusing on personalities and politics instead of performance. A real professional doesn't get personal or territorial. A true professional stays calm, logical, and focused on doing the best work possible for the team.

Benefit of the Doubt   Even if you start off not liking someone, a good team player will give another person the benefit of the doubt. You may rely on your first impression of a person, but first impressions can be wrong. If you are stressed out or having a bad day, you may not be the best judge of people. Reserve your judgment until you know the person better. Remember, you don't have to love your teammates; you just have to show respect for what they can do for the team. If a teammate turns out to be a gossip, then distance yourself from that person. Do your best to make sure that he or she does not affect your work.

Preventing Conflict

Once you understand some of the causes of conflict, you can take steps to prevent them. It is difficult to change a person's attitude, but sometimes a bad attitude takes a while to develop. People can have negative **tendencies** or poor work habits. These tendencies can get worse when people are under stress or when they are dealing with personal problems. If you know someone has a tendency to slack off, address the issue.

tendency an impulse to act a certain way

- Have a team meeting about acceptable work standards.
- Don't single out a person. Make it clear that no one on the team should be doing careless work.
- Remind everyone that you depend on each other and that you're all working toward the same goals.

All Eyes on the Goal

At the first signs of conflict, remind people why you are working together in the first place. By keeping your mind on the team's goals you will be less likely to get involved in arguments and squabbles. This solution also works well for people who have a tendency to get personal about disagreements or who spend more time gossiping than working. Have a meeting, get the team together, and remind them why you are there: to do business.

> *Whenever anyone has offended me, I try to raise my soul so high that the offense cannot reach it.*
>
> *René Descartes*
> *French Philosopher*

Team Building

In some companies, entire departments are devoted to building stronger teams. Seminars, staff meetings, and conferences teach teammates how to work together. For example, teams may work together building houses as a community service project or sponsoring a soapbox derby for local kids. These events focus on team building in a fun, low-pressure environment, teaching the skills needed to work effectively in a team: trust, equality, respect, and understanding.

Managing Confrontation

All team members should work to prevent conflict, but you also should know how to resolve a conflict. You have read that the primary cause of conflict is lack of respect. Misunderstanding happens when there is a breakdown in communication between team members. Sometimes people misinterpret an action, believing they've been treated with disrespect when, in fact, they haven't. People can forget their communication skills under pressure. They may become so focused on what they have to do that they forget to be considerate of others.

The Effects of Stress

Tensions can run high and tempers can become short when people are under pressure. During stressful times, it is especially important to keep a cool, calm, professional attitude. People who forget to communicate, or who get short and snappish because of stress, can cause misunderstandings. To resolve this type of problem,

- Define the conflict.
- Find out details of the specific incident that started the conflict.
- Speak to everyone involved—together—and clear up the misunderstanding.
- Encourage everyone to move forward.

Most importantly, people will be careful not to make the same mistake next time they are under pressure.

The Effects of Anger

Tempers that get too hot can lead to destructive confrontation. Confrontations usually happen when people are fed up with disrespectful or negative behavior. They lose their tempers. Instead of confronting the offending person in private and in a calm and professional way, an angry person may blow up and say hurtful or disrespectful things. That person is not thinking logically. Once those words are said, they cannot be taken back. They can be forgiven, teammates can work out problems and move on, but most people don't forget it when they have had their feelings hurt. It is best to avoid arguments or unplanned confrontations.

Walking Away   As an adult there are more important things than proving you are right. The people who matter—your boss and teammates—will judge you by how you handle yourself. Even when someone is really pushing your buttons and trying to provoke a fight, you should always be the bigger person. Walk away, if that's what it takes to avoid confrontation. If you walk away, you show that you are putting the team first and are a cool-headed professional. Once everyone has calmed down, you can sit down and sort out your problems and get back to work.

Mediation

With more difficult conflicts, it's sometimes necessary to use a process called mediation. In **mediation** someone—usually someone outside of the conflict—steps in to help resolve the issue.

The outsider is known as a mediator. A mediator acts like a referee at a sports event. Mediators keep everyone focused on resolving the problem. They are there to make sure people who want to resolve a conflict stick to the rules. They make sure conflicting parties do not get emotional or personal or say unfair or unhelpful things. If you have a conflict with another person, a good solution is to choose someone you both respect to mediate your dispute. If you cannot agree on a mediator, pick someone you both feel is **impartial.** A mediator can be someone from outside your team or department, but it is best to resolve the conflict by involving as few people as possible. Before you can start mediating a conflict, both parties have to agree to accept the mediator's decision to end the conflict, even if they don't like it. By making this agreement, you are compromising.

Compromise

Compromise occurs when conflicting parties each gives up something in order to reach an agreement. It is necessary for building any good relationship, personal or professional. When a conflict arises, you need to be willing to make a **concession,** which means giving up something so the other person can meet you halfway. The other person does the same. Concessions can involve admitting some of the fault for

> **"** In the stress of modern life, how little room is left for that most comfortable vanity that whispers in our ears that failures are not faults! **"**
>
> *Agnes Repplier*
> *Author and Social Critic*

> **"** Always do right. That will gratify some of the people, and astonish the rest. **"**
>
> *Mark Twain*
> *American Author and Humorist*

mediation a process where an outside party is brought in to help resolve a conflict

impartial to be unbiased and not take sides

compromise when conflicting parties each gives up something in order to reach an agreement

concession what a conflicting party agrees to give up in order to reach a compromise

Tips From a Mentor

Conflict Management

Here are ten tips to help you keep your cool during workplace conflicts:

- **Stay out of it.** Don't take sides or try to solve someone else's problem if it doesn't involve you.

- **Don't take the bait.** If provoked into a confrontation, take a deep breath, stay calm, be professional, and walk away.

- **Think before you speak.** Say your piece without blaming or attacking. If you say something you regret, it can never be taken back.

- **Listen before you respond.** Don't be defensive; hear someone out before you disagree.

- **Be honest and show integrity.** Admit it if you're wrong, and take responsibility for your words and actions to help solve a conflict.

- **Be professional, be polite,** and don't tolerate anything less. If a situation gets nasty, respectfully remind people of their manners.

- **Remove yourself from a tense situation.** Take a walk during lunch, hit the gym, or grab a coffee in a quiet corner. Clear your head and try to maintain an objective perspective.

- **Discuss the problem, not the person.** Avoid character assassination by not bringing up past mistakes, personalities, or prejudice in a conflict.

- **Be the voice of reason.** Always keep discussions practical and to the point, focusing on what you can do, not what was done.

- **Move on.** Accept an apology, resolve a conflict, and avoid bitterness and resentment.

a misunderstanding or accepting an equal amount of blame. By doing this, you and the other person stop worrying about who was right and who was wrong. You both admit to some of the responsibility for the conflict so that you can move on and begin resolving it. Teammates should try to compromise unless it is a case where one person clearly does something wrong or intentionally provokes a fight. If you compromise, smaller conflicts can usually be resolved without mediation.

Official Action Legal action should be considered as a last-resort option. The lowest level of conflict resolution is usually the best not only for an organization, but also for the individual. However, very rarely, a conflict can become so intense that it starts to involve whole teams or departments. In that case, you may have to take some kind of official or legal action to resolve it. This usually only happens when the conflict involves an accusation of a crime, or a really bad deed.

Thinking Critically Mediation is one of the options for resolving conflict in a team. *What qualities should a good mediator have?*

Finding Solutions

With most conflicts, you are going to want to find the quickest and simplest solution. If the conflict can be worked out between the people involved without bringing others into it, good. Working out problems with teammates should always be the first choice because it is less disruptive to other members of the team. When everyone involved in a conflict listens and communicates effectively, misunderstandings can be resolved easily.

QUICK RECAP 2.4

NEGOTIATING AND RESOLVING CONFLICT

- Teammates can politely and constructively disagree; it happens all the time. But when someone thinks you are being disrespectful to him or her, a small disagreement can grow into a bigger conflict.
- Confrontations usually happen when someone is fed up with disrespectful or negative behavior and loses his or her temper.
- Even when someone is really trying to provoke a fight, you should always be the bigger person. If you walk away, you show that you are putting the team first and are a cool-headed professional.
- If you are in a conflict with another person, choosing someone you both respect to mediate your dispute is a good solution.

Internet Quest

Headline News

Look up any combination of the words *arbitration, mediation, conflict, negotiation,* or *concession* on the search option of the news site. List three examples of conflict resolution in business or world affairs.

You also can **research** topics using the search engines www.yahoo.com, www.google.com, and www.lycos.com. Remember, one of your best sources for information on teamwork is www.mhhe.com/pace.

- When a conflict arises, you need to be willing to make concessions, which means giving up something so the other person can meet you half way.
- In every conflict, you should find the quickest and simplest solution.

CHECK YOURSELF

1. List one of the biggest causes of conflict in a team.
2. Name an ability that is essential to resolving conflicts.

Check your answers online at **www.mhhe.com/pace.**

 Pace ONLINE

BUSINESS VOCABULARY

conflict   a sharp disagreement in interests or ideas
tendency   an impulse to act a certain way
mediation   a process where an outside party is brought in to help resolve a conflict
impartial   to be unbiased and not take sides
compromise   when conflicting parties each gives up something in order to reach an agreement
concession   what a conflicting party agrees to give up in order to reach a compromise

Working Effectively with Others

Once a team has established goals and is working without conflict, there is no end to what it can achieve. Through the collaborative efforts of its members, a team can increase efficiency and productivity. With the skills to keep a team running smoothly, your team is ready to take on some real challenges. With a strong sense of trust and respect in place, an organized team can solve most problems.

Facing Tough Challenges When we talk about solving problems through teamwork, we mean something different than overcoming the kinds of interpersonal conflicts we talked about in the last section. While pursuing your goals as a team, you will face significant challenges. For example, you may not have enough money to complete a charitable project and, therefore, may have to think of a creative way to raise funds. You may work on a task force to implement a new computer program, so you'll have to learn complicated new systems. Whatever the challenge, when your team is ready and working, you can use the skills, talents, and ideas of everyone on the team to come up with the best solution.

The Decision-Making Process

The decision-making process a team uses can vary depending on how a team is structured. Teamwork is about sharing responsibility, but most teams will employ some form of leadership. Team leaders are usually project managers, and they are in charge of overseeing all team functions. Team leaders keep the team's goals in sight and make sure that each member is completing his or her action steps.

Think of a team leader as the conductor of an orchestra. Each musician in an orchestra may play his or her own part successfully, but the conductor is needed to bring all the parts together to fully realize the music. Depending on the business and the team setup, the leadership of a team may or may not have the final say when it comes to making decisions.

The most frequent approaches to decision making in a business setting are listed below. Each approach has strengths and weaknesses.

- Imposed decisions
- Majority rule
- Unanimous decision
- Build a consensus

Imposed Decisions

When you were a child, how did you and your friends, as a group, decide whether to play kickball or dodge ball? If the three oldest kids in the group chose to play kickball, and that became the decision for the group, that decision was an "imposed" decision. In this case, the people with the most authority or power—the big kids—would make the decision and impose it on the others. This is a fast way to reach a decision, but it isn't necessarily fair—or popular with people who want to play dodge ball.

Majority Rule

majority more than half

Another option would be to make a **majority** or popular decision. If more than half the kids on the team voted for kickball, then the group would play kickball. This system is much more democratic, but it still leaves a big group of unenthusiastic dodge ball fans.

Unanimous Decision

unanimous in complete agreement

To avoid the "tyranny of the majority," you might hold out for a **unanimous** decision, one where everyone agrees to play kickball. This is the best solution because everyone is happy and ready to play the game. However, getting everyone to agree is tough enough on the playground, but it's even harder in the business world.

Build a Consensus

consensus general agreement based on the best option

Often the best solution is to build a **consensus.** This is an agreement the whole group comes to after considering all the options. The decision is then made based on which option makes the most sense. So, as kids, even though the majority of the group wanted to play kickball, and the big kids were for it, someone mentioned that it was about to rain. So you talked it over as a group and reached a consensus to play dodge ball, because you didn't have the room to play kickball inside.

To reach a consensus, everyone on a team has to know how to compromise. Remember that compromising means everyone gives up something in order to meet halfway. When a team comes to a consensus, everyone will be more likely to accept the decision. Good team leaders can help a team reach a consensus by pointing out the pros and cons of all the options. To reach a consensus you also have to be able to collaborate, or work together.

So remember the three Cs of group problem solving:

- Collaboration
- Compromise
- Consensus

When you collaborate, you make compromises so that you can reach a consensus.

> **❝** *Where all think alike, no one thinks very much.* **❞**
>
> *Walter Lippman*
> *Pulitzer Prize-Winning Author*
> *and Columnist*

Collaborating on Problems

Collaboration among teammates goes beyond just making decisions. It is an important way we find solutions to problems. Team leaders may have the final say on a team decision, but they are not solely responsible for solving team problems. When teammates collaborate on a problem, several people—not just one or two—search for a solution.

The Power of the Fresh Perspective

The brain power of several people combined is powerful because different people have different ways of looking at things. Each person approaches the same problem from a different perspective, and may see different solutions. Have you ever worked

Figure 2.5 *Learning to Trust*

Thinking Critically How can trusting your teammates improve your work environment?

on a word puzzle where you have to find the word in a big group of random letters arranged in columns and rows? You think you've found all of the words, then a friend comes by and takes one look at the puzzle and points out three words you hadn't noticed. Your friend isn't necessarily smarter; he or she just has a fresh perspective. That's why collaborating on team problems works. When one person gets stuck in a way of thinking, someone with a fresh perspective may point out something that was missed.

Trust, Confidence, and Respect

As you learned in Section 2.1, you can't have teamwork without collaboration, and you can't have collaboration without respect and trust. When someone trusts your judgment, he or she has confidence in your abilities. With that confidence comes respect. A team cannot get to a point where members are collaborating if team members don't have confidence in each other. Everyone can benefit when a team works well together (see Figure 2.5). Learn to trust your teammates. If you have concerns, discuss them with the person responsible. However, approach the topic in a way that shows you are confident in your teammate's abilities and respect that person's contribution to the team.

Maintain Your Integrity

It is definitely easier to build trust among team members when everyone is **reliable.** Completing assignments and arriving for work and meetings on time helps to establish you as someone who is reliable.

    Keeping your word by delivering on promises also proves you're reliable. Most importantly, maintaining your **integrity** in every situation shows that you are trustworthy.

    If you do your work and live your life with integrity, your teammates will respect you. When so much of the success of a team depends on each person's contribution,

reliable a person or thing that can be depended upon

integrity honesty, sincerity, and morality

Teamwork

Your Challenge

You are reviewing a presentation that you and your teammates are due to give at the next team meeting for the department management. You realize that a number of statistics are incorrect. This was information that one of your teammates was supposed to gather. This isn't his first mistake. His work has been substandard lately, and correcting this error will put your whole group a day behind on preparing the presentation. What should you do?

The Possibilities

A. Ignore the mistake; make the presentation and hope no one notices.

B. Wash your hands of him. Take the mistake to your team leader and request his transfer.

C. Show him the mistake, ask for an explanation, and correct it regardless of the deadline.

D. Just make the corrections yourself and get on with the meeting.

Your Solution

Choose the solution that you think will be most effective and write a few sentences explaining your opinion. Then check your answer with the answer on our Web site: **www.mhhe.com/pace**.

> *Honest differences of views and honest debate are not disunity. They are the vital process of policy-making among free men.*
>
> *Herbert Hoover*
> *31st President of the United States*

it is important that you never let your teammates down. Integrity means different things to different people, but it always includes

- Honesty
- Sincerity
- Effort
- Respect

Doing Good Work

With the team organized, teammates collaborating without conflict, steps planned, and problem-solving strategies outlined, your team can get some serious work done. It is important to make the most of all the team's resources, including time.

Team Meetings

You can keep team meetings productive by preparing an agenda for each meeting. Start with a *progress report* from each section of the team. Each group can update the team on projects they're working on, talk about any problems they are having, and ask for help from the team. Then the team can *review the minutes* of the last meeting to get a sense of their overall progress and adjust their goals or deadlines. After you discuss all of your issues, you can then *decide upon the team's next plan-of-action steps* and determine who will be assigned each step. Stick to the agenda and avoid conversations that don't relate to the project. Team meetings can be social and have a casual, conversational tone, but that should not keep you from covering all the points on your agenda.

Evaluating Work

When you trust and have confidence in your teammates, it is much easier to exchange ideas and evaluate work. No one likes to have work criticized or have mistakes pointed out, but when someone you trust is making suggestions, you know it is not personal. Your teammate is only making suggestions to help you improve the quality of your work and to help out the team. Conflict arises when people can't take friendly suggestions or criticism. Trust your teammates. This leaves you free to make suggestions and improvements that would keep the work of the team at a high standard.

We can rely on our teammates to check for minor oversights, typos, factual errors, or other important details. We also can use our teammates as sounding boards by trying out ideas and rehearsing presentations with them. It is very easy to make little mistakes when we spend a lot of time working on a project. We can be too involved in what we are doing to have a fresh perspective. Like an artist who takes a step back from a painting in order to see the whole picture, a teammate's fresh perspective can help to produce the highest quality work. Creating and maintaining this standard of excellence is one of the responsibilities of a team.

Team Spirit

Working on a team is not just about getting the job done well; it also can be a lot of fun. We get to share our triumphs and disappointments with others. We get to meet and share ideas, talk and brainstorm, work together, and laugh together. When we finish a project, we also can enjoy a sense of accomplishment together. There is something very satisfying about a job well done, and it is an even sweeter feeling when we can share it with others.

QUICK RECAP 2.5

WORKING EFFECTIVELY WITH OTHERS

- The decision-making process a team uses can vary depending on how a team is structured.
- When a team comes to a consensus, everyone will be more likely to accept the decision.
- Each person approaches the same problem from a different perspective, and thus each may see different solutions.
- So much of working together is learning to trust another person to do a job right.
- If you do your work and live your life with integrity, your teammates will respect you.
- You can keep team meetings productive by preparing an agenda for each meeting.
- A teammate's fresh perspective and insight can help to produce the highest quality work possible.
- Creating and maintaining this standard of excellence is one of the responsibilities of a team.
- There is something very satisfying about a job well done, and it is an even sweeter feeling when we can share it with others.

CHECK YOURSELF

1. Name the most effective method of decision-making for a team.
2. List three abilities that are essential to group problem-solving.

BUSINESS VOCABULARY

majority   more than half

unanimous   in complete agreement

consensus   general agreement based on the best option

reliable   a person or thing that can be depended upon

integrity   honesty, sincerity, and morality

Chapter Summary

2.1 The Importance of Teamwork

Objective: *Define the role and importance of teamwork in the business world.*

In this section you learned that teamwork has been around since the earliest civilizations and is an essential part of modern business. Teamwork increases worker efficiency and productivity. Teamwork benefits everyone because all team members share a common goal. Team members collaborate to ensure the team's success.

2.2 Where Teamwork Starts

Objective: *Explain and use the individual skills needed to be a productive team member.*

In this section you learned that teamwork starts with you. The modern business world is diverse, so in order to be a good team player, you must show respect for your teammates. You learned that you can do this by listening carefully and communicating clearly, by being flexible, and by showing tolerance and understanding. By practicing your individual teamwork skills, you will set the standard of behavior for the team.

2.3 Organizing a Team

Objective: *Organize yourself and your team, identify goals, and take action.*

This section taught you the value of an organized approach to life and work. You learned how to organize team goals by planning and prioritizing action steps and how to organize team members according to function. You also learned that when planning action steps, you need to think about "How to . . . ." and "What is needed to . . . ." You found out that a good team should have project managers, schedule managers, information managers, financial trackers, and a communications function.

2.4 Negotiating and Resolving Conflict

Objective: *Identify, address, and prevent conflict among team members.*

In this section you learned how to overcome conflict on a team. You learned that conflict is caused by negative or unprofessional attitudes, and that you can prevent it by addressing these tendencies in yourself and others. You also learned that in order to resolve conflict through mediation, team members need to be able to compromise and make concessions.

2.5 Working Effectively with Others

Objective: *Collaborate with teammates to solve group problems and accomplish goals successfully.*

This final section taught you that by bringing together the skills in Sections 2.1 through 2.4, you can really start accomplishing goals as a team. You learned that the best way for teams to make decisions is by reaching a consensus. You reexamined the ideas of collaboration, trust, and respect, in terms of working together to solve problems as a team. Most importantly, you saw that teamwork can be fun as well as effective.

Business Vocabulary

- action steps (p. 58)
- adapt (p. 53)
- aptitudes (p. 62)
- attributes (p. 56)
- categorizing (p. 56)
- collaboration (p. 48)
- compromise (p. 67)
- concession (p. 67)
- conflict (p. 64)
- consensus (p. 72)
- diversity (p. 53)
- efficiency (p. 45)
- impartial (p. 67)
- integrity (p. 73)
- long-term goal (p. 57)
- majority (p. 72)
- mediation (p. 67)
- motivation (p. 48)
- prioritize (p. 60)
- productivity (p. 45)
- reliable (p. 73)
- responsibility (p. 48)
- short-term goal (p. 57)
- tendency (p. 66)
- tolerance (p. 53)
- unanimous (p. 72)

Key Concept Review

1. Give one reason why working in a team is more effective than working on your own. (2.1)

2. What is the difference between efficiency and productivity, and how are these ideas related? (2.1)

3. What does diversity in the workplace mean? (2.2)

4. Name three ways you, as an individual, can show respect for your teammates. (2.2)

5. When you prioritize action steps, how should you arrange them? (2.3)

6. Which function on a team is responsible for outlining and prioritizing action steps? (2.3)

7. List one quality needed to mediate a conflict. (2.4)

8. What do you have to be able to do in order to compromise and resolve conflicts? (2.4)

9. What is the least effective and most unpopular method of making a decision when working on a team. (2.5)

10. Name one benefit of working as a team to solve group problems. (2.5)

Online Project

Team-Building Exercises

Use a search engine to research team-building activities or exercises. Find out which companies employ these exercises. Use your research to write a one-page presentation on an exercise of your choice. Explain the exercise and then demonstrate it to your class. Get everyone involved.

Step up the *Pace*

CASE A   *Plan a Meeting*

The company you work for is planning a big marketing meeting with their branch offices, and your department has been assigned the task of organizing it. Your branch will be hosting 100 people from all over the country for two nights. The company employees will arrive in the afternoon and there will be a welcome banquet the first evening. The next day starts with a group orientation meeting, followed by seminars with guest speakers throughout the afternoon and a presentation in the evening. The next day consists of seminars followed by a final group meeting. Your team leader has asked you to be responsible for finding a hotel or conference center to host the meeting at a reasonable price.

What to Do

1. Outline and prioritize your action steps for researching and booking a location for the meeting.

2. Brainstorm a list of other topics that need to be considered when planning this type of meeting.

CASE B *Workplace Stress*

Your best friend happens to be someone you work with, and you know that she is going through some personal problems at the moment. You realize that your friend is bringing that stress into work, is not concentrating, and is snapping at others. You try to tell your friend what you have noticed, but she flies off the handle. Your friend accuses you of being jealous of her career and trying to sabotage it. She complains to your team leader, saying that you are impossible to work with because you are overly critical, negative, and not a team player. You know this is not true and want to set the record straight at work, but you are afraid that your friend will get personal and that you will lose the friendship.

What to Do

1. Think of the best way to address this conflict and get back to work.

2. Compose a draft of a letter to your friend and teammate stating how you would like to resolve the conflict.

Logical Order

Most sentences are arranged according to an order, or structure. This helps communicate ideas clearly. Order is particularly important when giving instructions or directions. To communicate information effectively, make clear connections based on a logical order. Words such as *first, next, then, following,* and *finally* all help to communicate steps in an order.

Which paragraph below makes the most sense?

1. Melt the butter in the frying pan. Scramble eggs in a bowl, adding milk as you mix. Pour the egg mixture into the pan. Serve the eggs when cooked thoroughly. Turn the stove burner to high. Put a frying pan on the stove. Stir the eggs when they begin to bubble.
2. First scramble eggs in a bowl, adding milk as you mix. Next, put a frying pan on the stove. Turn the stove burner to high. Melt the butter in the frying pan. Then pour the egg mixture into the pan. Stir the eggs when they begin to bubble. Finally, serve the eggs when cooked thoroughly.

The best answer is paragraph 2. The directions are more clear in paragraph 2 because the words *first, next, then,* and *finally* help communicate the proper order.

Exercise: On the lines provided, write a paragraph using the following sentences in a logical order:

- I got dressed, putting on jeans and a sweater for the cold weather.
- I cleaned the snow off my car before driving to work.
- I had a cup of coffee before I went outside.
- I took a hot shower.
- I got up, slowly, to a cold house.
- I dried off, combed my hair and brushed my teeth.

Become a Leader

What Will You Do?

3.1 Understanding Leadership Dynamics Examine the relationship between leaders and teams; learn what it takes to create a positive leadership dynamic.

3.2 Modeling Leadership Recognize the qualities, environment, and style of effective leaders, and learn how to model yourself after them.

3.3 Cultivating Trust and Respect Learn the importance of trust and respect in leadership and how to build it with your team.

3.4 Identifying Leadership Responsibilities Examine the different administrative and managerial tasks of successful leaders.

3.5 Thinking Strategically Learn to turn your ideas into a leadership vision and develop a strategy for making your vision happen.

Why Do You Need to Know This?

The difference between having a job and making a career is the desire to challenge yourself, to always learn more, and to become better at what you do. As you grow and perfect your professional skills, you will be given more responsibility in your work. You may eventually get to a point where you are responsible for others. This is what it means to be a leader. To prepare for this opportunity you need to learn what it means to lead, and how to lead with vision and style.

Explore a World
OF FINANCIAL POSSIBILIT

Chapter Objectives

After completing this chapter, you will be able to:

- Explain how a leader creates the balanced relationships needed to maintain a positive leadership dynamic.

- Create a leadership model and develop the necessary qualities, environment, and style to become an effective leader.

- Lead in a way that earns the trust and respect of your team, builds their confidence, and motivates them to do great work.

- Identify leadership responsibilities, delegate tasks, handle promotions and dismissals, make decisions, manage, and motivate effectively.

- Develop a leadership vision, test it, and present a proposal to make your vision happen.

Set the *Pace*

Leadership Think about your past experience with leadership. Did you have a boss or teacher you respected as a leader? Did you work with someone whom you did not respect as a leader? Have you ever been in a position of leadership on a sports team, in a community group, or at school?

Activity In the journal section of your career portfolio, write two or three paragraphs explaining what qualities you look for in a good leader and what you think makes a bad leader. Also write about the challenges you faced when you were in a leadership role. Share your thoughts with your classmates during a discussion about the importance of setting standards.

Understanding Leadership Dynamics

Everyone has the potential to be a leader. Leaders aren't made simply from charisma, good looks, the right degree, or the right job. These things help, but to understand leadership, you need more than a winning smile. Even born leaders have to learn and develop skills to allow them to lead effectively. Most of these skills you have already learned by developing a standard of excellence and being a team player. Right now, you have the raw materials it takes to become a leader. You only need the desire to lead and an understanding of leadership dynamics.

Lead the Way   There are many ways you can lead: by doing a good job, setting a positive example, or volunteering your time to worthy causes. Leadership doesn't come with a job assignment. Leaders make the job. If you have the desire to be a leader, you can develop your natural leadership potential by understanding what leadership is and how it works.

Reading and Study Tip

Word Study
The word *dynamic* is used as a noun in the phrase *leadership dynamic*. Find a place in the text where it is used as an adjective and explain the difference.

authority the power given to judge, act, or command

❝ *The leadership instinct you are born with is the backbone. You develop the funny bone and the wish bone that go with it.* ❞

Elaine Agather
American Businessperson and CEO of JP Morgan Chase, Dallas

manage to run, handle, or direct a system, task, or person

motivate to encourage someone to act

leadership dynamic the pattern of changing systems and relationships that occur between leaders and the people they lead

What Makes a Leader

Authority means the power given to judge, act, or command. Company leaders give the people in management positions the authority to make decisions. This authority comes with the job and is what separates a manager from other employees. What separates leaders from managers is how they use their authority.

The Three M's

A good leader uses his or her authority to do three things:

- Motivate
- Manage
- Make decisions

Leaders make decisions about their team's goals, action steps, and their priorities. Leaders make decisions on behalf of their entire team or department. To implement these decisions, a leader has to know how to manage. To **manage** means to run, handle, or direct a system, task, or person. Leaders need to plan and administrate action steps, assignments, budgets, resources, and staff in order to implement decisions. Most managers can do both of these things quite well. What makes a leader, though, is the ability to motivate. To **motivate** means to encourage someone to act. A successful leader uses his or her authority to motivate a team to meet their goals by doing great work.

Leadership Dynamics

To successfully motivate your employees, you need to understand your relationship with them. A **leadership dynamic** is the pattern of changing relationships that occur between leaders and the people they lead. Because leaders have authority, they have the power to tell their employees what to do. However, that authority alone is not going to motivate employees to go the extra mile for a leader. To be a good leader, you need a positive leadership dynamic. A positive leadership dynamic occurs when a leader's authority is respected and employees are happy to follow his or her lead.

Boss or Buddy

Leadership styles can greatly affect a workplace. Read the following example to find out how. Marissa and Catherine are both managers at a clothing outlet and are responsible for the sales staff. Both are having trouble with their staff's performance and can't figure out why.

Marissa thinks her employees don't like her and are purposely doing bad work. They spend more time chatting with each other than they do pushing for sales. When she gives them orders, they roll their eyes and whisper comments as she leaves the room. They don't listen when she reprimands them for mistakes and sloppiness. A couple of people have even quit without giving notice. Her staff members don't seem to realize that she is the boss. She is there to make them perform, not to chitchat about weekend plans.

Catherine feels that her employees don't respect her authority. She tries to be a cool boss by being understanding when staff arrive late or visit with friends in the store. She gets along well with everyone, but some clerks are taking advantage of her friendship. They show up very late and slack off too much. When she confronts them, they give her all kinds of excuses, promise to do better, but don't keep their promises. She has threatened to fire them, but she knows she could never fire a friend.

What's The Problem? For your employees to respect your authority, you have to find a balance between being a boss and a buddy. Employees want to be respected as teammates and treated in a friendly, understanding way. They won't work hard for someone who barks orders at them. However, leaders need to set boundaries and keep discipline. Employees may like a boss who is friendly and understanding, but if they can get away with poor performance, they won't be challenged to work hard.

Follow the Leader

Not everyone has the desire to be a leader. Many of us are happy concentrating on what we're good at and leaving the big decisions to someone else. This means that there are always people willing to follow a leader. When your employees respect your authority, they recognize you as the leader and take you seriously. However, people only put their fate in the hands of a leader whom they trust and respect. To motivate people to follow your lead, you have to make them *want* to follow you.

Leadership Roles

Marissa Is Only the Boss	Catherine Is Only a Buddy
Marissa needs to be more friendly and encouraging to her staff.	Catherine needs to assert her authority to her staff.
She is the boss, but is too bossy.	She is their buddy, not their boss.
This leads to resentment.	This makes her a pushover.

Trust and Respect

To have a positive leadership dynamic with your employees, they have to respect you as a professional and trust you as a person.

You earn respect:
By your performance as a professional and as a leader
You earn trust:
By looking out for the interests of the team and by behaving well as a person

To gain the trust and respect of your employees, you need a combination of skill and ability in your job, and skill and ability with people. It doesn't matter how good you are at your job; if you are selfish and can't get along with people, you can't lead. In turn, you may be charming and popular with everyone at work, but if you don't know your job and can't do it well, you can't lead others to do theirs. Trust and respect go hand in hand. You don't respect someone you don't trust and you definitely don't trust someone you don't respect. To be a good leader, you need both trust and respect from the people you lead.

Building Balance

There is no formula for being a good leader. You can't do x, y, and z to guarantee leadership success, but you can work to create a positive leadership dynamic. Creating a positive leadership dynamic is all about finding balance (see Figure 3.1).

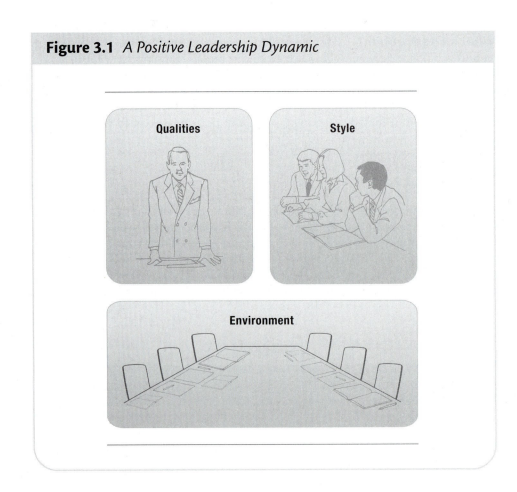

Figure 3.1 *A Positive Leadership Dynamic*

Qualities

Style

Environment

New Attitudes / New Opportunities

Meet Javier Robles and Janus. Janus is Javier's service dog assigned to assist Javier on the job. Javier earned a graduate degree in Law. Javier is currently the Deputy Director for the New Jersey Division of Disability Services, in Trenton. Here's what Javier has to say about . . .

What He Considers Leadership Qualities   "To me, leadership means showing that you have the ability to make things better for other people. You need good leadership skills like fairness and assertiveness without aggressiveness. You should treat everyone equally and respect different viewpoints. This makes people feel like part of a team, like you have their interests at heart and are helping them to advance. Also, know your industry and educate the people that work with you about its issues, professional and otherwise."

Learning Leadership Skills in Other Places   "You get leadership skills from your job, but you also learn leadership skills from other activities. If you are involved in an organization or you do volunteer work, you can gain leadership skills just by being involved. These organizations may put you in charge of events or people. You might not get paid for it, but you're making decisions that affect other people—that's great experience!"

How to Deal with Challenges As a New Leader   "Some people get bogged down in their failures. When you start doing that, it's easy to give up. It's a lot better to ask yourself, 'What am I doing right?' and 'What skills or qualities do I bring to this job?' Build on all those positives as opposed to the negative. Especially as a person with a disability, you really have to think about all the things you *can* do, because you have enough people around you thinking about all the things you *can't* do. It's important as a disabled person or as a minority to realize that you bring a perspective that others don't have."

We will discuss ways to do this later in the chapter, but for now it is important to understand how all these different factors work together.

Leadership Vision

What defines a leader is his or her **leadership vision.** Your vision is what you and your team want to accomplish, and the way you want to accomplish it. As a leader, you are in a position to bring fresh ideas into an organization, to make yourself heard, and to change things. You have the authority, the following, and the talent to take risks and make changes. You have the opportunity to do things the way you and your team think that they ought to be done. To be a great leader, you need a vision of what those changes will be. The best way to motivate your team is to share that vision with them. Bring them on board and ask them to help you make your vision of a better workplace a reality. There is no better motivation than everyone working for something that they believe in.

leadership vision the ultimate goal or outcome a leader directs his or her team toward

> *I believe that you get greater effectiveness in your work when you tie people's personal mission with the corporate mission.*
>
> **Richard Barrett**
> *Former Values Coordinator for the Word Bank*

Dynamic Leadership

Now that you understand the balance you need in order to have a positive leadership dynamic, you can get to work building that balance. In the next sections, we will show you how to achieve this balance and how to motivate, manage, and make decisions as a leader.

UNDERSTANDING LEADERSHIP DYNAMICS

- A leader has the authority to make decisions and direct employees.
- A good leader makes decisions, manages, and, most importantly, motivates.
- Leadership dynamics are the changing systems and relationships that occur between leaders and the people they lead.
- To have their authority respected, leaders need to be both a boss and a buddy.
- Not everybody wants to lead, but everyone does want leaders they can trust and respect.
- Earn respect through your skills as a professional; earn trust through your actions as a person.
- Trust and respect go hand in hand.
- You create a positive leadership dynamic by maintaining a balance between your professional skills and your people skills.
- You can motivate your team by having a leadership vision, sharing it with them, and helping them adopt it.

CHECK YOURSELF

1. What separates a good leader from a simple manager?
2. As a leader, should you try to be a boss or a buddy to your employees?

Check your answers online at **www.mhhe.com/pace.**

BUSINESS VOCABULARY

authority   the power given to judge, act, or command
leadership dynamic   the pattern of changing systems and relationships that occur between leaders and the people they lead
leadership vision   the ultimate goal or outcome a leader directs his or her team towards
manage   to run, handle, or direct a system, task, or person
motivate   to encourage someone to act

Modeling Leadership

Have you ever walked into a meeting at a new company and picked out the boss without anyone telling you who he or she is? What about this person gave you the impression that he or she was in charge? In today's business world, you can't assume someone is in charge because of his or her age, gender, or race. Instead, you look for the sense of confidence and authority that comes from being a leader. Good leaders don't have to remind people that they are in charge. Their authority is demonstrated by their image, their actions, and their employees' attitudes towards them. It is important that people view you as a leader. If you have to spend your time enforcing your authority and proving that you're the boss, you won't get much else accomplished.

Take Me to Your Leader To build the right image as a leader, you need to think about the kind of leader you want to be, and then work to lead that way. All of us have role models—people who have qualities we respect and try to copy. In business, you can model yourself on the qualities that make an effective leader. With this image in place, people will mark you for a leader by your air of *authority* and the respect that your colleagues give you.

Effective Leadership

An effective leader is measured by the success of the team that he or she leads. A successful team works efficiently together and has high productivity. To be a good leader, you have to make sure your team members are motivated and happy. Examine Figure 3.2.

Leadership Model

How does a successful leader achieve these positive results? You know that you have to maintain a positive leadership dynamic, but where do you start? Start by creating a leadership model, outlining the basic qualities you need to lead effectively.

Leadership Qualities

Leadership qualities are the personal traits that can help you be a good leader. Figure 3.3 shows a list of various personal qualities. Choose the qualities you think you have as a potential leader.

Kinds of Leaders

Each column in Figure 3.3 lists qualities that belong to a certain kind of leader. Which column did you most often choose from?

- Column 1 is the *instinctive leader,* who relies on natural leadership ability to lead.

Reading and Study Tip

Connotation
Connotation is the impression attached to a word's definition. For example, *childish* and *childlike* mean the same thing, but *childish* has a negative connotation. Find a pair of similar words with different connotations in this section. Explain the difference between the words' meanings.

Figure 3.2 *The Measures of an Effective Leader*

Team Works Well Because	How You Know
Employees are happy at work	No bad behavior, disrespect, frequent resignations, or transfer requests
Employees are motivated to work	No long lunches, absenteeism, distraction with personal calls, e-mails, or games
Employees do good work	No mistakes, sloppiness, half-hearted jobs, need for reprimands, or close supervision
Employees do teamwork	No competitiveness, conflict, or secrecy; responsibility and resources are shared
Employees do inspired work	Sharing of new ideas; knowledge capital used for the team's benefit

Team meets goals on time and on budget

Motivated to set new goals

Thinking Critically Every team should strive to be efficient and productive. *How does the performance of a team reflect on its leader?*

- Column 2 is the *structured leader,* who relies on structure, rules, and tradition to lead.
- Column 3 is the *spontaneous leader,* who relies on creative energy and new ideas to lead.
- Column 4 is the *skilled leader,* who relies on practiced leadership skills or training to lead.

Leadership is about balance. There are no set rules for what makes a good leader, but most successful leaders can draw on several qualities to help them lead. Not every employee will respond to one type of leader. If you have an employee who is insecure and you are an instinctive leader who uses humor to motivate, this person may not respond well to your style. In this case, you need sensitivity as well. The skilled leader finds a compromise between all these qualities. Here, the leader may use optimism to encourage a sensitive team member. Leaders start with the qualities they already have and adopt other qualities to create a well-rounded, professional leadership style.

Work Environment

Atmosphere can impact how employees work. Even if you like your job, an unpleasant work environment can kill your motivation. Instead of working, you watch the clock until you can escape the office and go home. However, if you think of your

Figure 3.3 *Leadership Qualities*

Column 1	Column 2	Column 3	Column 4
Personality	Creativity	Control	Confidence
Humor	Sensitivity	Reserve	Optimism
Courage	Understanding	Firmness	Patience
Good looks	Personal style	Formality	Professional image
Talent	Ability	Aptitude	Skill
Honesty	Sincerity	Frankness	Integrity

Thinking Critically Marks of good leadership can be classified in four categories. *Which qualities do you respect in a leader? What do they have in common?*

office as a place where you can be social, exercise your mind, and do great work, you can get excited about your job. Is coming to work a pleasure or a punishment for your employees? It is up to you, as a leader, to create an environment that allows employees to work well.

The climate in your office is a reflection of you as a leader. If it is frosty and uncomfortable, employees, visitors, and customers will assume the person who runs the department is the same. Your behavior will set the ability to set the climate in your work environment. You can create a fair climate by encouraging, not enforcing.

Fair or Frosty You want to create a climate in which employees feel comfortable—a place where they can work without tension or constant supervision, but still have the support of rules and structure. The climate in your department should be fair, not frosty.

Frosty Environment	Fair Environment
Unfriendly and serious	Friendly and light
Too formal	Formal or casual, but respectful
Tense and unpleasant	Relaxed and pleasant
Too strict and structured	Flexible but responsible
Controlled and uncreative	Spontaneous and creative
Intimidating	Encouraging
Unpleasant, uncomfortable, unproductive environment.	Pleasant, comfortable, productive environment!

❝ The best executive is the one who has sense enough to pick good men to do what he wants done and self-restraint to keep from meddling with them while they do it. ❞

Theodore Roosevelt
26th President of the United States

❝ I am a man of fixed and unbending principles, the first of which is to be flexible at all times. ❞

Everett Dirksen
U.S. Politician and Republican Senator

Turn up Teamwork Encourage your team members to use their independent knowledge, express themselves, set their own goals, and work as a team. Guide them, instead of enforcing your authority to control them. No one does their best work when they are micro-managed. To **micro-manage** is to overmanage an employee by frequently meddling, supervising, and making unneeded corrections. This creates tension and limits productivity. As long as team members are delivering quality work on time, you can trust them to make their own choices instead of enforcing rules you make. This creates a fair climate and immediately informs employees of what kind of leader you are trying to be.

Leadership Style

Your leadership style is how you use your power and authority to lead. There are many different styles of leadership. Here are some examples:

- Based on power and control:
  - Autocratic: giving orders without allowing employees to participate.
  - Formal: hands on.
- Based on respect and trust:
  - Democratic: involving your team in leadership through discussion and voting.
  - Casual: hands off.

You need to choose a style that fits with your leadership qualities and the environment you created as a leader. You should be so skilled in your qualities that you can deal with different kinds of people effectively. Your environment should be comfortable because you respect employees' independence.

So, your style should be flexible. This way you can satisfy employees who need hands-on attention, while respecting the need of others to work on their own. This is the style of leadership you use to create a positive leadership dynamic. This is how you go about interacting with people and motivating them. To find a balance between boss and buddy, you need a balance between an autocratic, hands-on, bossy style and a democratic, hands-off, buddy style (see Figure 3.4).

Communicate Your Style

The best way to communicate your leadership style is to lead by example. Let your actions do the talking for you. You can tell your employees about your great qualities and flexible style all you want; they will be convinced by what you do, not what you say. Remember your individual teamwork skills from the last chapter? They include:

- Being respectful.
- Listening carefully.
- Communicating clearly.
- Being flexible.
- Showing tolerance and understanding.

It is even more important for you to practice these skills as a leader. Show your team what kind of leader you are and what you expect from them by setting an example in your everyday actions.

Communication Style

As a leader, you spend much of your time communicating instructions, directions, ideas, and critiques to others. When you communicate as a leader, you have to do two things: make your communication clear, and communicate with authority.

Figure 3.4 *A Leadership Model Completed*

Confidence, optimism, patience, professional image, skill, integrity

Flexible leadership style

Comfortable work environment

- **Clear communication means** *content:*
  - Think about what you are going to say before you say it.
  - Isolate your point and make it; avoid tangents or subjects that are off the point.
  - Commit to your words and sentences; avoid ifs, buts, maybes, and I guesses.
  - Do not talk just to hear yourself speak.
  - Tailor your words to your audience.

- **Communicating with authority means** *delivery:*
  - Speak clearly, without uhhs, umms, wells, likes, and you knows.
  - Make eye contact and have a friendly face for your listeners.
  - Use gestures to illustrate a point; avoid fidgeting or covering your mouth.
  - Speak slowly and deliberately so listeners understand you.
  - Spit it out; don't indulge in dramatic pauses or waste your listeners' time.

Contribution and Confidence   Communicating as a leader is about making a valuable contribution by confidently saying what you mean. In a meeting, people should stop and listen because they want to hear what you have to say. They won't listen just because you are the boss. Being a leader is not about talking the loudest or jumping in first with your comments. A leader listens, makes choices about what to say, and says it with confidence.

> *It is no exaggeration to say that a positive self-image is the best possible preparation for leadership in life.*
>
> **Dr. Joyce Brothers**
> *American Psychologist, Columnist, and Author*

Putting It Together

Once you have created your leadership model, you can begin modeling yourself after it. When you know which qualities you have, which ones you want to develop, and what kind of environment you want to create, you have everything it takes to be an effective leader. If you practice this model of leadership, you will become a role model for your employees. Your employees will be motivated to follow your positive example, copy your qualities, and be better team members.

QUICK RECAP 3.2

MODELING LEADERSHIP

After this section, you should know how to create a model of the type of leader you want to be. Here's a summary of some of the things you learned:
- A leadership model allows you to create the image you want as a leader by isolating what makes an effective leader.
- A leader's effectiveness is measured by the success of the team he or she leads.
- A leadership model deals with your qualities as a leader, the environment you create, and your style of leadership.
- Effective leaders practice skilled leadership, create a comfortable office climate, and have a flexible style.
- Leaders need to communicate their style clearly and with authority.

CHECK YOURSELF

1. What leadership style should you try to have?
2. What does a leader need to think about in order to communicate clearly?

Check your answers online at **www.mhhe.com/pace.**

BUSINESS VOCABULARY

micro-manage   to overmanage by frequently meddling, supervising, or making unneeded corrections

Cultivating Trust and Respect

Leadership does not happen without trust and respect. A boss may be able to bully and intimidate employees into doing what he or she says, but they will do just enough to get by. As an effective leader, your employees will work for you because they know that you are all working together. When employees trust and respect their leaders, they will go the extra mile for them. They will share their vision and they will give their leaders something no bully will ever get—loyalty.

All for One AND One for All   Loyalty means faithfulness. A good leader has the loyalty of the people he or she leads because he or she puts the team and its members first. To gain loyalty from those you lead, you need to gain their trust and respect by being a supportive and genuine leader. If you can build a loyal team, you will have the support you need to take risks and make a difference as a leader.

Gaining Trust

To gain your employees' trust as a leader, you must prove to them that you won't abuse your power or authority. They should be confident that you will not use your position of leadership to boss and bully, but rather to guide them to do better work. They need to trust that you will always act with integrity, you will look out for each team member, and that you will be a good person as well as a leader. You gain this trust by being a supportive leader. Supportive leaders put the interests of their employees before their own. This leader makes sure employees' needs are met so they can work safely and comfortably. More importantly, this leader encourages his or her employees to think beyond their basic needs to develop themselves as potential leaders.

Moving on Up

Amy is packing up her desk on her last day of work. She is headed for a new job as a manager at a different company. She is relieved to finally be making a move forward, especially after working for a boss that didn't support her or her teammates. She decides to use her boss as a model of how *not* to lead in her new job. She thinks of every instance where he was unsupportive and makes a decision to do the opposite for her employees.

During her first week in her old job, she made a request for a better chair and a desk lamp so she could work at her computer more comfortably. Her boss told her that those items weren't necessities, and that if she asked for special equipment, everyone would want it.

1. Amy decides that her first goal as a leader will be to make sure everyone on her team has what he or she needs to work comfortably.

When she took night classes sponsored by her company to earn a certificate in management, she was asked to work on a big presentation. She was due to present

---

Reading and Study Tip

Acronyms

An *acronym* is a word that is formed from the first letters of a series of words in a phrase. To help you remember its meaning, you can turn a word into an acronym using phrases that describe the word. Look for the acronym in this section. On a separate sheet of paper, make an acronym out of your name using words that describe you.

Leadership is a potent combination of strategy and character, but if you must be without one, be without the strategy.

General Norman Schwartzkopf
General in U.S. Army

---

it to the class and needed time to set up. She asked her boss if she could leave 15 minutes early. He told her that she had to stay because her extra-curricular activities shouldn't affect her job.

2. Amy decides that if her employees are motivated to learn new skills, she will do whatever she can to support them.

When she felt restless in her old job, she asked her boss for advice and permission to take on some new, more challenging assignments. Her boss told her he thought she was great at her current job and he needed her to stick to that.

3. Amy decides that if her employees feel that they aren't being challenged, she will give them the opportunity to try new things so they can grow as professionals.

The week before she got married, all of her co-workers pitched in and bought her a cake to say congratulations. Her boss thought it was her birthday. He didn't even know she was engaged.

4. Amy decides that she will make the effort to get to know her employees as people, not just workers. She will support them in their lives and careers.

Last month, her department was behind on a project because they were under-staffed and needed some help. They asked their boss to bring in a temp until they got caught up. He refused because he didn't want to risk being overbudget and up-setting the regional manager. The whole team worked overtime, but still received a talking to from the regional manager at the end of the month. Their boss didn't say a word in their defense.

5. Amy decides that she will stick up for her team, get them what they need, and defend their work ethic no matter who complains.

A+ for Amy

There is no doubt that Amy will earn the trust and respect of her team. These decisions aren't only good for individual team members; they are also good for business. Here's why.

1. Taking care of employees' basic needs such as comfort, safety, and salary, takes their minds off these issues and allows them to focus on doing great work.
   • Result: higher productivity and efficiency.
2. Encouraging employees to keep learning their profession means that you will have highly skilled team members who know how to do better work with less supervision.
   • Result: higher quality work.
3. Giving employees the opportunity to make progress will keep them motivated and working for you. If you pigeonhole an employee in one job, he will have nothing to gain by working harder.
   • Result: higher motivation and less turnover.
4. Getting to know your employees shows that you respect them as individuals who have lives outside of work. Also, if they have personal difficulties that are affecting their work, you will be able to address their performance.
   • Result: higher trust and increased ability to handle employee problems.
5. As a leader, you are your employees' representative to upper management. You prove your loyalty when you stick up for them and praise their

accomplishments. You are showing that you won't wash your hands of them if things get tough. Disowning your team when it is struggling is the worst thing you can do as a leader and as a professional. If your team fails, you fail.

- Result: loyalty from your team.

Gaining Respect

Respect and trust go hand in hand. As a leader, the trust of your team comes from your actions as a person. Respect comes from your actions as a professional. To be respected as a professional, you need to be knowledgeable and skilled at your job, and use your authority as a leader in a professional way. As a leader, you have the power to assign work, make decisions, resolve conflict, and direct behavior. A professional does not use this authority to lighten his or her own workload. You can't expect your team to work hard for you if you are not willing to work hard yourself. You can't expect to mediate conflicts if you are at the center of them. You also can't expect employees to be honest if you are not honest yourself. Because good leaders lead by example, your example has to be impeccable.

Example is not the main thing in influencing others. It is the only thing.

Albert Schweitzer
German Nobel Prize–Winning Doctor and Humanitarian

Do As I Say AND As I Do

Impeccable means faultless or beyond reproach. Here are some ways you can set an impeccable example:

- Be smart. Your decisions and actions affect your team, so be smart about what you do.
- Be fair. When assigning work, giving praise, when resolving conflict, don't play favorites.
- Be real. Work as hard, put in the same hours, and do the same excellent job as your team.
- Be strong. Face challenges, tackle problems, handle crises, and overcome obstacles with courage.
- Be straight. Worry about the team, not your career; don't manipulate, exploit, or dominate.

Be Understanding, Be Approachable

Cultivating respect and trust will keep the lines of communication open between leaders and team members. Leaders need to be approachable so employees can come to them with problems, suggestions, and ideas. The boss who leads by intimidation will frighten his employees and, consequently, be the last to know if anything is wrong. This means that problems will only get worse.

Dealing with Resistance

The business world is a changing environment. As a leader, you can't rely on a formula or a single tried-and-true approach. Competitive business leaders take risks and use innovative ideas to stay ahead. To be **innovative** means to come up with new, inventive, original ideas. Even if you work hard to be a good leader, you may have people who hesitate to trust you and resist your leadership because it involves change.

innovative new, inventive, or original

Tips From a Mentor

Ten Ways to be Approachable

- *Leave your office door open* when you work.

- *Circulate amongst your employees,* saying hello and asking how people are doing as they work.

- *Use positive language* to respond to both good and bad ideas. For example, use phrases such as "That's a great idea" and "It should be developed further. Keep working on it."

- *When people present ideas* and problems, stop what you are doing, look them in the eye, and give them your full attention.

- *Take an interest* in each person. Ask after his or her family, schoolwork, hobbies, or appropriate nonwork activities.

- *Watch your body language.* Don't answer questions with shrugs; don't respond with grunts; don't stand over anyone in a dominating position.

- *Give employees the benefit of the doubt.* If they are ill or have personal problems, give them time to get caught up on their work.

- *Encourage* your employees to come to you with problems, questions, or ideas—and listen when they do.

- *Offer your advice,* guidance, and opinion to help employees develop professionally.

- *Reward good work* with praise, pizza for the office, a letter of recognition, or a simple thank you for hard work.

Pace Points

I Object

Sometimes employees resist a leader's idea. If this happens, state your case and listen to their objections. If you find you've made an oversight, admit it and thank them. If you still believe you are correct, thank them for their input and state politely that you would prefer that they try it your way.

Building Confidence

To influence is to sway or affect how a person behaves. Leadership is about influencing the people you lead to do what you think is best for the team. By setting a positive example, you are trying to influence your team to behave in the same way. When your employees trust and respect you, you become a major influence on them. If people resist your leadership, use your influence as a leader to build their confidence. Fear of change is common to a lot of people. People who resist innovative leaders are afraid that if the system or method of work they have mastered changes, they will no longer be good at their jobs.

What You Can Do   Remind employees that it is not one single piece of knowledge or skill that makes them a valuable employee. Be a mentor to these teammates by using your knowledge and skills to persuade them that change is good. Show them how they can be a part of that change by learning new and valuable skills that will allow them to grow towards a leadership position.

- M Motivate
- E Encourage
- N Nurture
- T Teach and train
- O Open eyes to possibility
- R Reward good work with praise

Lead to Believe, Believe to Lead

When you build confidence in your team and in each team member's individual ability, they will thank you by believing in you and your vision as a leader. When your team believes in you, you have their loyalty. When they believe in your vision, they have a personal investment in making that vision a reality. This means that each team member is motivated by personal belief and loyalty to work hard for a goal that you envisioned. When this happens, the people you lead truly become a team by sharing a goal and the personal and professional desire to achieve that goal. This is something that no bully, boss, or buddy can achieve; it takes a trusted and respected leader.

> " Leaders who win the respect are the ones who deliver more than they promise, not the ones who promise more than they can deliver. "
>
> Mark A. Clement
> Author

QUICK RECAP 3.3

CULTIVATING TRUST AND RESPECT

Here is another look at some of the ideas you learned in this section.
- Leaders who are loyal to their team will earn their team's loyalty.
- Loyalty is based on trust and respect.
- Trust is earned by your actions as a person; and respect is earned by your skill as a professional.
- As a leader, you have to set an impeccable example for your team.
- Leaders who are understanding and approachable will find out about problems and good ideas first.
- Resistance to a leader is usually caused by a fear of change.
- Leaders can deal with resistance by building the confidence of their team.
- When leaders build confidence in their employees, they build their employees' confidence in their leader.

CHECK YOURSELF

1. What kind of example should a leader set?
2. Why do many people resist the ideas of a new leader?

Check your answers online at www.mhhe.com/pace. *Pace* ONLINE

BUSINESS VOCABULARY

innovative   new, inventive, or original

Identifying Leadership Responsibilities

The last time you opened the classifieds, you probably didn't see any ads that read, "Wanted: Leader. Job responsibilities include being in charge, looking smart, and giving toasts at departmental dinners. Firm handshake and brilliant smile required." Being a leader is not about sitting back and taking the credit; it is hard work. A leader's main task is to create a vision and monitor and adjust the goals needed to achieve that vision. Dedicated leaders can never take their eyes off their goals.

The Buck Stops Here   Leaders ultimately take responsibility for the teams they lead. Everyone is responsible for his or her individual actions and decisions, but leaders have the final task of bringing those individual jobs together to meet goals. If a team fails, a leader fails. If a project isn't finished, it is because the team leader didn't make sure it was finished. If a goal is left unmet, it is because a leader didn't make sure it was met. A leader's job is to create a vision, figure out how to make it happen, and use skills, talents, influence, resources, and strength to fulfill that responsibility.

Reading and Study Tip

What It Means
As you read, look for references to "the big picture." Write a few sentences explaining what is meant by "the big picture."

delegate to assign or appoint someone the authority to carry out a task

❝ Don't tell people how to do things, tell them what to do and let them surprise you with their results. ❞

General George S. Patton
U.S. General and Tank Commander

capitalism a system where the means of production of goods and services are privately owned

profit the money made by selling goods or services after production costs have been subtracted

The Leader's Job

A good leader should know how to do the job of everyone he or she leads, but will never try to do all those things alone. Leaders can't do the work of others because they need to be free to focus on the larger issue of team goals and objectives. That is why good leaders delegate. To **delegate** is to assign or appoint someone the authority to carry out a task.

Two, Four, Six, Eight—This Is Why We Delegate

You know how to break down a goal into action steps. Leaders are in charge of setting ultimate goals, breaking them down into prioritized action steps, and then delegating a person or group to handle each assignment. Delegating tasks is like determining player positions. You want to delegate to the person or group that is best suited to a task.

The leader then becomes in charge of managing each group or person as they work to complete their assignments. The leader monitors the progress of each group, guides their work, and helps them address obstacles. As each group progresses, the leader readjusts their goals to ensure that all the teams are on the right track and will have their assignments ready to put together into a whole. All the while, the leader keeps an eye on the big picture, making sure his or her team goals fit with the goals of the company.

The Big Picture   You may be wondering what it means when people in business refer to the big picture. They are talking about viewing a business system or a company as a whole. In the United States, our economic system is known as capitalism. **Capitalism** is a profit-and-competition-driven system where the majority of goods and services are provided by privately owned and operated businesses. **Profit** is

Delegate

Your Challenge

You are a recently promoted manager with a reputation for doing precise, excellent work. You like doing things yourself, staying involved, and knowing the facts, but you can't keep up on your new workload. You are spending so much time trying to do every assignment perfectly that you cannot attend to the needs and goals of your team.

The Possibilities

A. Choose several people who do high-quality work and delegate to them important assignments that don't require your personal attention.

B. Make your favorite assignments a priority and hand the rest over to anyone who can get it done.

C. Delegate all your work to your team and spend your day having long lunches with management, playing golf, and discussing the big picture.

D. Do it all yourself and assign someone else to think about your team's long-term goals.

Your Solution

Choose the solution that you think will be most effective and write a few sentences explaining your opinion. Then check your answer with the answer on our Web site: **www.mhhe.com/pace.**

the money made selling goods or services after the production costs have been subtracted. The **production cost** is how much it costs for companies to produce the goods and services they sell. Capitalism is ruled by the economic idea of "supply and demand." According to the **law of supply and demand,** companies exist to supply goods and services that the consumer, or customer, demands. Companies compete to provide their services to more customers and increase their profit. When leaders look at the big picture, they look at how their goals fit with their company's goals.

Get to Work

A leader creates a vision and motivates his or her team to realize that vision. This is the most creative part of a leader's job. However, a leader also has to perform a number of different administrative and managerial functions. Let's take a look at some of the different tasks leaders perform on the job.

A Day in the Life

Joel is a sales manager at a national computer manufacturing company. His department has a staff of 25 employees who report to him. He and his team work to expand their sales territories, recruit new customers, manage the accounts they have, and keep customers by offering quality customer service. Here's his schedule for Monday.

Pace Points

Run with the Ball

Delegation involves trust. Once you hand an assignment to someone, step back and let him or her do it. Remember, leaders delegate so they can better use their time on larger issues. Pass a job to people who can do it best, let them run with the ball, and be surprised by their results.

production cost how much it costs companies to produce the goods and services they plan to sell

law of supply and demand economic rule that states that businesses exist to supply goods and services that the consumer demands

❝ Delegating work works, provided the one delegating works, too. ❞

Robert Half
Namesake of the Largest International Specialty Staffing Service

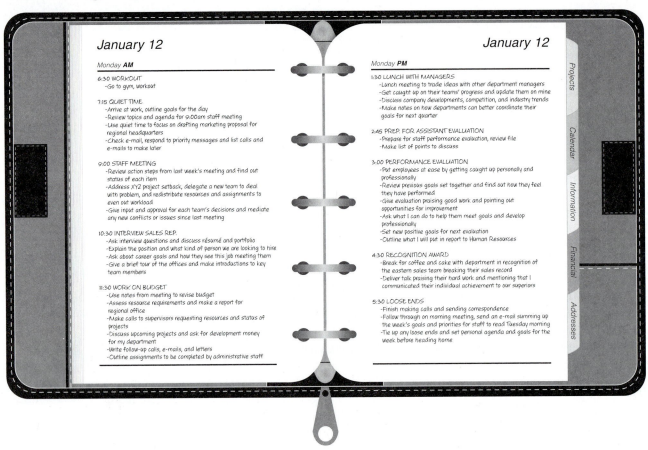

January 12

Monday AM

6:30 WORKOUT
- Go to gym, workout

7:15 QUIET TIME
- Arrive at work, outline goals for the day
- Review topics and agenda for 9:00am staff meeting
- Use quiet time to focus on drafting marketing proposal for regional headquarters
- Check e-mail, respond to priority messages and list calls and e-mails to make later

9:00 STAFF MEETING
- Review action steps from last week's meeting and find out status of each item
- Address XYZ project setback, delegate a new team to deal with problem, and redistribute resources and assignments to even out workload
- Give input and approval for each team's decisions and mediate any new conflicts or issues since last meeting

10:30 INTERVIEW SALES REP.
- Ask interview questions and discuss résumé and portfolio
- Explain the position and what kind of person we are looking to hire
- Ask about career goals and how they see this job meeting them
- Give a brief tour of the offices and make introductions to key team members

11:30 WORK ON BUDGET
- Use notes from meeting to revise budget
- Assess resource requirements and make a report for regional office
- Make calls to supervisors requesting resources and status of projects
- Discuss upcoming projects and ask for development money for my department
- Write follow-up calls, e-mails, and letters
- Outline assignments to be completed by administrative staff

January 12

Monday PM

1:30 LUNCH WITH MANAGERS
- Lunch meeting to trade ideas with other department managers
- Get caught up on their teams' progress and update them on mine
- Discuss company developments, competition, and industry trends
- Make notes on how departments can better coordinate their goals for next quarter

2:45 PREP. FOR ASSISTANT EVALUATION
- Prepare for staff performance evaluation, review file
- Make list of points to discuss

3:00 PERFORMANCE EVALUATION
- Put employees at ease by getting caught up personally and professionally
- Review previous goals set together and find out how they feel they have performed
- Give evaluation praising good work and pointing out opportunities for improvement
- Ask what I can do to help them meet goals and develop professionally
- Set new positive goals for next evaluation
- Outline what I will put in report to Human Resources

4:30 RECOGNITION AWARD
- Break for coffee and cake with department in recognition of the eastern sales team breaking their sales record
- Deliver talk praising their hard work and mentioning that I communicated their individual achievement to our superiors

5:30 LOOSE ENDS
- Finish making calls and sending correspondence
- Follow through on morning meeting, send an e-mail summing up the week's goals and priorities for staff to read Tuesday morning
- Tie up any loose ends and set personal agenda and goals for the week before heading home

Projects · Calendar · Information · Financial · Addresses

> ❝ A leader is best when people barely know he exists, when his work is done, his aim fulfilled, they will say: we did it ourselves. ❞
>
> *Lao-Tzu*
> Ancient Chinese Philosopher

multitasking working on more than one task at the same time

Dr. Joe Pace
LEADERSHIP

"The speed of the leader determines the speed of the pack."

Juggling Act

Leaders juggle many different responsibilities and tasks. It is very important that they stay organized and focused so that they can give their full attention to each new task. **Multitasking** is a phenomenon where you do more than one thing at the same time, like talk on the phone and search the Web. Multitasking allows leaders to be more efficient, but it also can also prevent them from giving one thing their full attention.

Leaders have to be careful that they don't burn themselves out or become too distracted to think clearly. Building quiet time into your schedule can help you stay focused on one thing at a time. Going to the gym and making time to assess personal goals also can also help keep leaders from burning themselves out. It is important that leaders have something left over for when they come home. Leaders need to balance their personal and professional lives so that they are content and have a balanced perspective. When you are tired or frazzled, you will not be able to step back and see the big picture.

Promotions and Dismissals

As the leader of a team, you are in a position to evaluate your staff's performance. This means that you can influence who is promoted or dismissed. There are many different circumstances that can bring about either fate, but there are a few key factors leaders should watch out for.

Dismissals

In the past, if someone lost his or her job, it was assumed that he or she was fired for doing something wrong. This is no longer the case. In uncertain economies, many employees are laid off due to budget cuts. As a leader, you may have to make decisions about who will be laid off. You also will also have to deliver the bad news. This is never a pleasant situation and is never easy. If you find yourself facing possible layoffs, ask yourself these vital questions:

- Can I rebalance the budget to cut costs and save jobs?
- Can I relocate this person to another department or position?
- Can I afford to lose this person's knowledge, skills, and personal contribution?

Layoffs are always a last resort and they are not a financial cure. In fact, layoffs can be quite expensive due to severance packages and legal fees. In turn, layoffs do damage to the morale of a team and compromise their trust and respect for you as a leader. This damage can be contained if your team and your employees know that you did everything in your power to prevent laying-off their colleagues.

Termination Due to Misconduct

You have already learned how to deal with misconduct as an individual and you know that as a leader you are ultimately responsible for your team. This means that as a leader, if misconduct does occur, you need to take action as soon as you are aware of it. Your job also is also to prevent and discourage misconduct among your team. Make sure your company's code of conduct is visible—meaning it is posted and has been circulated to all employees. Take time to explain the code and its implications to your staff, and remind them that you are always available to discuss problems before they become misconduct. If you are forced to dismiss an employee due to misconduct, make sure that

1. You have evidence of the misconduct.
2. You consult your human resources or legal department.
3. You follow your company's protocol.
4. You inform the employee in writing why he or she is being dismissed.

If you feel you cannot give this person a positive reference, warn him or her of this and state your reasons. This will protect you from legal action by former employees.

Promotions

Every employee needs an incentive to work hard. An **incentive** is an award or benefit that motivates us to act. Your paycheck may be your incentive for coming to work. For ambitious employees, more responsibility, greater challenges, and a bigger salary are the incentives for doing great work. Employees want to know that once they have proven their ability and paid their dues, they will be able to move up. This is the same reason you are learning how to grow as a professional right now. A better job is your incentive to pass this course.

As a leader, you are in a position to evaluate employees' work and recommend them for promotions. Promotions depend on budget, availability, and appropriateness. Not every promotion means a bigger paycheck. Promotions can be small steps that involve increased responsibility, prestige, or a new title and job function. Promotions should be based on merit, not popularity or favoritism. Everyone on your team should know that they have a shot at moving up the ladder by working hard.

incentive an award or benefit that motivates a person to act

Pace Points

Recognition is Promotion
Recognizing someone's hard work is like giving a mini promotion. It moves the person up in the eyes of his or her colleagues, and improves his or her self-esteem.

Tips From a Mentor

Qualities to Praise When Evaluating Employees

- **Professional behavior.** Are they too informal? Do they treat both colleagues and customers with respect?

- **Positive attitude.** Can they bounce back from setbacks? Do they look for the positive in situations?

- **Creative ideas.** Do they share new thoughts? Do they give unique solutions?

- **Promptness.** Do they arrive at work on time? Are their projects on time?

- **Independence.** Can they work on their own? Do they need constant supervision?

- **Initiative.** Do they find a need and fill it on their own? Do they assert themselves (without being too pushy)?

- **Willingness to ask.** Do they ask questions to clarify an assignment? Do they do complete a project incorrectly, later saying that they didn't understand?

- **Inspiring actions.** Do they set a good example for others? Do they encourage or inspire others to act?

- **A spirit of cooperation.** Do they share ideas? Do they work well with others?

- **Correct use of protocol.** Do they follow the proper chain of command? Do they follow the company code of conduct?

QUICK RECAP 3.4

IDENTIFYING LEADERSHIP RESPONSIBILITIES

- Leaders take the ultimate responsibility for the progress and success of their team.
- Leaders have the authority to delegate assignments and tasks to the team.
- Leaders are responsible for keeping an eye on the big picture to ensure that their team is headed in the right direction.
- In business, the big picture is how a team's work will help their company make a profit.
- Leaders need to be able to multitask without losing focus or doing poor work.
- Leaders have to thoughtfully evaluate staff for dismissals and promotions.
- Promotions give employees an incentive to do great work.

CHECK YOURSELF

1. What is the economic system of the United States called?
2. Name several incentives for employees to work hard.

BUSINESS VOCABULARY

capitalism   a system where the means of production for goods and services are privately owned

delegate   to assign or appoint the authority to carry out a task

incentive   an award or benefit that motivates a person to act

law of supply and demand   economic rule that states that businesses exist to supply goods and services that the consumer demands

multitasking   working on more than one task at the same time

production cost   how much it costs companies to produce the goods and services they plan to sell

profit the money made by selling goods or services after production costs have been subtracted

Thinking Strategically

You! Yes, you, reading this book, right now. Are you still following along? This is a lot of information, but don't stop yet. All your hard work and follow through on the previous chapters is going to pay off, because in this section you get to be in charge. Why are you working so hard in school? Why are you are spending so much time learning? Because you have great ideas! Take charge and use your personal knowledge, skills, and great ideas to create a leadership vision. You have the power to make a huge difference as a leader. Chances are, you've made some mistakes or had mixed-up priorities in the past. You might have learned a few lessons the hard way, but you still learned enough to move forward. You are starting fresh, believing in yourself, going back to school, and putting your hard-earned knowledge to good use. You have worked very hard to make it this far, but don't stop here.

Wanted: Principal for School of Life   Use your experience to create a vision of how things can be done differently and better. Use your valuable and unique skills, talents, and understanding to make it easier for those who follow in your footsteps. Create a vision to lead the way for your colleagues, employees, family, friends, community—and for yourself.

Reading and Study Tip

Commands

As you read, pay special attention to sentences or phrases that are worded as commands. For example, "Read this book." List several commands and write a sentence stating what they are telling you to do.

> ❝ *Some men see the world as it is and ask why; others see the world as it might be and ask why not.* ❞
>
> *George Bernard Shaw*
> *Irish Nobel Prize-Winning Playwright and Social Commentator*

inspire to stir emotion, drive, or intellect as a means to motivate

aspire to aim for or hope to achieve

The Power of Vision

When you hear the term *vision,* you might think of those dial-up psychics on TV having visions of your future and past. A leadership vision does not require a crystal ball, but it is a look into the future—the future as you see it. Your leadership vision is how you picture your goals in your mind, like a daydream or a mental image.

Your Personal Vision

What do you see for yourself when you finish school? Is it a vision of a better, more satisfying job, a higher salary, and a better quality of life? When you made your decision to go back to school and you informed your friends and family, how did you convince them that the time and hard work would be worth it? What was it that you said to motivate them to support your decision? You described that vision of a better future. You showed them the possibilities, told them what realizing those possibilities would take, and asked for their support.

Inspire, Aspire

Imagine if leaders like Abraham Lincoln and Martin Luther King, Jr. hadn't envisioned an America where all people were free and equal. Both Lincoln and King communicated their vision of a brighter future in powerful speeches meant to inspire people. To **inspire** means to stir emotion, drive, or intellect in order to motivate someone to act. To **aspire** to something means to aim for or hope to achieve it. Vision is a powerful tool for leaders because when you envision your goal, you can communicate it. You can describe to others what you see in your mind to others so they can see it too. Your vision gives you a goal to aspire to and a picture of an ideal to inspire others. An **ideal** is a principle or a perfect model of an idea. If you can inspire people to share your ideal and vision, they will aspire to help you make that vision a reality.

Developing Your Leadership Vision

Your leadership vision includes your goals for your team. Your vision reflects your unique style, manner, values, and ideals as a leader. Others may have similar goals, but how they envision reaching those goals will be different. Your vision should be what directs all the decisions you make as a leader.

What Is Your Vision

No one can tell you what your leadership vision will be. It depends on you and what you want to accomplish. You should think about what your ideals are as you determine your vision. What do you want to improve and how can you, with your unique style and background, make things better? Ask yourself:

- What do I know about my job?
- What do I know about my team?
- What do I know about my company?
- What do I know about my industry?
- What do I know about society?

What don't I like in all of this and why?
What can I do to make it better?

ANSWERS = IDEAS = VISION

Assess your knowledge and look for patterns, common obstacles, drawbacks, and flaws in how things are done. Think of how you can improve them.

What Do You See?

Turn your ideas into a statement of your vision. Describe what you see in one sentence or phrase. For example: *I see our department becoming recognized for high-quality customer service.* When you have a vision statement, you can start to flesh out the whole vision. To **flesh out** means to add substance (such as details) to the framework of an idea. Put some meat on the bones of your idea by thinking about how and why. Here is our example developed further: *I see our department becoming recognized for high-quality customer service by developing a more efficient method for processing customer returns while working to lower their number. This will increase customer satisfaction and will help us retain the customers we have while giving us something to offer new customers.*

Where Do You Start?

Vision is about determining an end result and working backwards to figure out how to make this goal happen. It's like knowing a destination to which you want to travel to, without yet knowing how you will get there. You tackle your vision like you tackle any other goal: by outlining and prioritizing action steps, and figuring out how to accomplish each step. Having a vision gives your action steps direction. As you start to carry out each step, always make sure that it is moving you in the right direction. Make sure you have clearly defined and developed your leadership vision statement. If your vision is unclear or keeps changing, your goals and priorities also

Dr. Joe Pace
GOALS

"No one can predict to what heights you can soar. Even you will not know until you spread your wings."

ideal a perfect principle or model of something

Internet Quest

A Leader's Vision

Search for the text of Abraham Lincoln's Gettysburg Address and Martin Luther King's famous "I Have a Dream" speech. Read their words and write two or three paragraphs stating the ideals and vision of each great leader.

flesh out to add substance to or further develop an outline or idea

Communicating a Vision

Your Challenge
You have been on the job as a leader for three months and feel like you know the direction your department needs to take. You have a clear vision, but it's risky and will scare off many of your more established team members.

The Possibilities
A. Just forget about your vision and ask your superiors for instructions.

B. Sit down and outline your vision. Make a presentation that you think your team will understand and try to win their support before moving forward.

C. Take your idea straight to the head of the company and wing it. Convince this person of your vision using just your powerful personality.

D. Spend all your time and team resources testing and researching your vision and forget about everything else until you get it approved.

Your Solution
Choose the solution that you think will be most effective and write a few sentences explaining your opinion. Then check your answer with the answer on our Web site: www.mhhe.com/pace.

will also be unclear. You will not be able to communicate your vision consistently. This will make it impossible for your team to understand what you are trying to achieve.

Thinking Strategically

As a leader, people follow you. You are like an explorer leading the way to new and exciting destinations. Sometimes, those destinations are unknown and frightening, lands where no one has been before. Sometimes to achieve an innovative vision of an ideal future, you have to take risks. As a leader, this means that your team has to follow you into unknown territory and be willing to take those risks with you. Any time you take risks, you have to show people that you have a strategy for success.

Communicating Your Vision

When you take risks, you are gambling with success or failure. You take risks because the possible rewards of success motivate you to take a shot at achieving your vision or goal. To be a great leader, you have to be willing to take risks and challenge the status quo to move your team and company forward. **Status quo** means accepted beliefs or standard practices. There is nothing wrong with the status quo—it is safe and reliable—but if Christopher Columbus hadn't challenged the assumption that the world is flat, we wouldn't be here today. As you know, change and new ideas frighten many people. If your vision challenges the status quo, you need a strategy for communicating it to your team and superiors to convince them your idea will work.

> ❝ A leader takes people where they want to go. A great leader takes people where they don't necessarily want to go but ought to be. ❞
>
> *Rosalynn Carter*
> *Mental Health Advocate and Former First Lady*

status quo commonly accepted belief or standard practice

Test Your Vision

Your superiors probably lead the way in developing what is now considered the status quo, which you are now challenging. This means that they have personal pride attached to the status quo. Great leaders won't let their ego stand in the way of a great idea, but they have to be convinced that it is a great idea. Your superiors only want to hear about great ideas that are focused, thoroughly developed, and possible. If your vision is based on change, you need to be sure that you have thought it through carefully before you present it to others. You can do this by testing your vision.

Vision Cross-Examination If you watch courtroom dramas on TV, you know that when a lawyer cross-examines witnesses, he questions them forcefully to find holes in their stories or faults with their ideas. When you present a risky idea to your superiors, they will do the same to you. Before they approve any vision, they will question you to find out how well you have developed your ideas. They want to know the following:

- **What is the benefit of your vision?** Will your vision save money, increase profit, increase productivity and/or efficiency, increase business, or defeat competitors?
- **What are you basing your case on?** Do you have research and data to prove your idea can work? Have other businesses used a similar idea effectively?
- **Can you make it happen?** Do you have a strategy for achieving this vision? Have you thought of the pros and cons of your idea? Do you have ways of dealing with the cons? Do you know what you need and how to get it?

Your Vision Statement

You need to have answers for all of these questions before you can convince your superiors of the benefits of your vision. Before that, however, you have to convince your team. Share your vision statement and ask for their feedback. See what they think: Are they inspired, and will they aspire to make this happen? If so, recruit their help in answering the cross-examination questions. Delegate members of your team to help you find answers to these questions and prepare a proposal for your superiors.

Presenting a Proposal

Once superiors say no to a proposal, it is very hard to get them to change their minds. Convince your superiors to say yes by presenting them with a thorough, organized, well-researched proposal. A **proposal** is a report that lists your developed vision statement and addresses cross-examination questions before they are asked. There are three strategies you can use to help get your proposal approved:

1. **3D Vision.** Use three-dimensional models, slides, charts and graphs, graphic designs, **prototypes** (nonworking models of a product) or any other visual aid to bring your idea to life.
2. **Best Practice. Best practices** are ideas that other industries or competitors use successfully. Demonstrate how your vision can incorporate and build on these best practices to beat the competition. This fuels your leaders' competitive spirit, which is a strong motivator.
3. **Negative Option.** This is a way to give yourself your superiors' approval before receiving official approval. Follow through on your proposal presentation with a memo thanking your superiors for their attention. Use this memo to highlight the positive suggestions they made and outline the

Pace Points

A Piece of the Pie
When teammates work on a vision from the beginning, their input helps develop it. This gives them ownership of the vision and motivation to see it succeed. When it does succeed, they share the credit.

proposal an idea presented for approval

prototype nonworking models of a product

best practices ideas that other industries or competitors use successfully

steps you are planning to take to implement those suggestions. Unless they respond saying, *no, wait,* or *don't do anything,* you give yourself their permission to get started.

Looking Ahead

Once you have your vision developed, your team inspired and invested in it, your strategy in place, and the approval of your superiors, nothing can stop you. You have become a true leader, with the skills, ideas, and courage to make a difference. When you get to the stage where you can develop a vision and make it happen, not only have you arrived as a leader, but also as a professional. Use your leadership position to explore unknown areas in your career and life. Find opportunities, make things happen, and make things better for you, your team, and tomorrow.

QUICK RECAP 3.5

THINKING STRATEGICALLY

At this point, you have learned most of the skills you need to be an effective leader; you just have to develop your vision. Here's what this section discussed about strategies for achieving that vision.

- A good leader should have a vision of what they want to accomplish and how.
- You can use your own unique perspective and background to inform your leadership vision.
- You should be able to inspire your team and give it something to aspire to with your vision.
- You can turn your ideas into a vision by expressing them as a vision statement.
- Visions that involve change from the status quo can be frightening, so you need to have a clear idea about your vision and its risks.
- Before you present your vision, you should test it by answering all the cross-examination questions that might be asked at a pitch meeting.
- When you present your vision as a proposal, use visual aids, do your research, and give yourself permission to get started.

CHECK YOURSELF

1. How do you use your vision to motivate people?
2. List the steps you should take once you have created a vision.

Check your answers online at **www.mhhe.com/pace.** *Pace* ONLINE

BUSINESS VOCABULARY

aspire   to aim for or hope to achieve

best practices   ideas that other industries or competitors use successfully

flesh out   to add substance to or further develop an outline or idea

ideal   a perfect principle or model of something

inspire   to stir emotion, drive, or intellect as a means to motivate

proposal   an idea presented for approval

prototype   nonworking model of a product

status quo   commonly accepted belief or standard practice

Chapter Summary

3.1 Understanding Leadership Dynamics

Objective: *Explain how a leader creates the balanced relationships needed to maintain a positive leadership dynamic.*

In this section, you learned that a leadership dynamic is the relationship between a leader and the people he or she leads. A leader's job is to make decisions, manage, and motivate. To do this successfully, you need to develop a positive leadership dynamic. You create this dynamic by being professional yet personable and by cultivating trust and respect.

3.2 Modeling Leadership

Objective: *Create a leadership model and develop the necessary qualities, environment, and style to become an effective leader.*

In this section, you learned to use the characteristics of a successful leader as a model and to use your authority as a leader to develop your natural and skilled leadership qualities.

3.3 Cultivating Trust and Respect

Objective: *Lead in a way that earns the trust and respect of your team, builds their confidence, and motivates them to do great work.*

This section talked about the importance of trust and respect in leadership. You found that it is loyalty that makes employees go the extra mile for a leader and that loyalty has to be earned. Leaders can earn the trust and respect of their employees through their actions as a person and as a professional. Leaders can build loyalty within a team by being loyal to the team.

3.4 Identifying Leadership Responsibility

Objective: *Identify leadership responsibilities, delegate tasks, handle promotions and dismissals, make decisions, manage, and motivate effectively.*

This section covered the various administrative and managerial responsibilities of a leader. You learned that leaders have to delegate work so they are free to adjust goals and guide their team. Leaders have to keep an eye on the big picture in order to keep their team moving in the right direction.

3.5 Thinking Strategically

Objective: *Develop a leadership vision, test it, and present a proposal to make your vision happen.*

This final section taught you about turning your ideas into a leadership vision. You learned that your vision is the individual contribution you make as a leader. It is a way for you to use your influence to bring about improvements and change. You learned how to develop, test, and propose your vision to your team and superiors. You also learned strategies for earning approval so you can begin to make your vision happen.

Business Vocabulary

- aspire (p. 106)
- authority (p. 84)
- best practices (p. 109)
- capitalism (p. 100)
- delegate (p. 100)
- flesh out (p. 107)
- ideal (p. 107)
- incentive (p. 103)
- innovative (p. 97)
- inspire (p. 106)
- law of supply and demand (p. 100)
- leadership dynamic (p. 84)
- leadership vision (p. 87)
- manage (p. 84)
- micro-manage (p. 92)
- motivate (p. 84)
- multitasking (p. 102)
- production cost (p. 101)
- profit (p. 100)
- proposal (p. 109)
- prototype (p. 109)
- status quo (p. 108)

Review of Key Concepts

1. How should good leaders use their authority? (3.1)

2. What is the best way to motivate your team? (3.1)

3. What is the benefit of creating a comfortable working environment? (3.2)

4. When you micro-manage an employee, what are you doing? (3.2)

5. What can a leader do to build employee confidence? (3.3)

6. What does a supportive leader do to gain the trust of his or her employees? (3.3)

7. How do smart leaders handle their workload? (3.4)

8. Name a big incentive for employees to do good work. (3.4)

9. What should you do after you develop a vision statement? (3.5)

10. What can you do to help explain your vision when making a proposal? (3.5)

Online Project

Living Like a Leader

Chose any historical or modern figure who is known as a leader. Research his or her life and find two examples of moments when he or she demonstrated leadership ability. What can you find out about his or her style and qualities as a leader? Print a picture of this person, write two paragraphs about his or her life and work, and make a list of his or her leadership qualities. In class, make a brief presentation describing the person, his or her life, and what qualities contributed to his or her leadership style.

Step up the *Pace*

CASE A   *Recognition*

Your team has just finished a complicated project. You managed to make all your deadlines and deliver your project on budget. A lot of people worked overtime to make this happen and, as their leader, you want to say thanks. They really have done a great job and deserve some recognition.

What to Do

1. Think of three ways you could show your appreciation to your team and pick the one you would like the best.
2. Write a paragraph about what you would plan, and another two paragraphs in the form of a speech detailing what you would say to thank your team for their hard work.

CASE B   *Leadership Vision*

You have a great idea for a new product. You have everyone on your team on board and have thought it through carefully. You are ready to make a proposal to your superiors, but you are nervous that they will say no. You have done all your research and know you have a great idea. You know that this idea could make the way your company runs better for years to come, but you are still scared about taking a risk. You just aren't sure if the heads of your company will listen to your idea. You can't decide what to do.

What to Do

1. Think about why you are scared to make your proposal and how you can overcome your fear.
2. Make a list of the pros and cons of taking risks to achieve your vision. Write a paragraph explaining ways you can build support for your idea.

Voice Mail

Using the phone in business differs greatly from using the phone socially. The phone should be used as a communication tool. You should always be prepared to leave a brief, but detailed, message. You should write yourself notes detailing what you want to communicate; or even write a short script for yourself.

Which message is the most professional?

1. "Oh hi, Lauren. I was really hoping to catch you. Please call me back as soon as you can. Thanks, bye. By the way, this is Steven. Bye."

2. "Hi, Lauren. This is Steven in Accounting. I'm calling to find out the status of the ABC account. If you can, please e-mail or call me by the end of the day at extension 553. Again, that's 553. Thanks."

3. "Hi, Lauren. This is Steven Duffy in Accounting. I'm Taylor's assistant. I'm calling in regards to the ABC account—especially invoices 21345 and 21363, which seem to be overdue. Please call me back at extension 553 by 11:00. Don't call between 10:00 and 10:30; I'll be in a meeting then. Talk to you soon."

Choice B is the most professional message. He gave just the right amount of information, including who he was, why he was calling, and how to get back to him. Choice C actually gave too much information, while A gave too little. Also, in choice A, Steven was obviously not prepared to leave a clear message. After receiving message B on her voice mail, Lauren can prepare to find the information Steven needs when she contacts him.

Exercise: Write your own script to leave on someone's voice mail. Practice saying it so that your message will be pleasant and clear enough to understand.

_____
_____
_____
_____
_____
_____
_____
_____
_____
_____
_____
_____
_____
_____
_____
_____
_____
_____

Glossary

A

accountable responsible or answerable for a person, action, or thing

action steps the specific tasks your team needs to complete in order to achieve a goal; the fundamental jobs or tasks necessary to realize any goal

adapt to change to suit new circumstances

aptitudes natural abilities, tendencies, or talents

aspire to aim for or hope to achieve

asset a valuable possession

attributes characteristics that describe a person or thing

authority the power given to judge, act, or command

B

best practices ideas that other industries or competitors use successfully

C

capital wealth or resources in the form of money or property

capitalism a system where the means of production for goods and services are privately owned

capitalize on benefit from or use to your advantage

categorizing grouping thing according to their common attributes

collaborate work together

collaboration the act of working together, combining talents and skills

compliance to comply or obey

compromise when conflicting parties each gives up something in order to reach an agreement

concession what a conflicting party agrees to give up in order to reach a compromise

conflict a sharp disagreement in interests or ideas

consensus general agreement based on the best option

credibility trustworthiness and believability

D

delegate to assign or appoint the authority to carry out a task

discipline strict control that enforces compliance

diversity variety of different people, ideas, or things

E

efficiency the ability to complete a task without wasting time, materials, or energy

ethics a system of morals and behavior

F

flesh out to add substance to or further develop an outline or idea

G

globalization the opening up of world markets to allow countries to freely trade goods, services, labor, and capital

H

harassment any form of constant torment or bothersome behavior that singles out an individual in an uncomfortable or upsetting way

I

ideal a perfect principle or model of something

impartial to be unbiased and not take sides

implement to put into effect

incentive (1) a reward or source of motivation; (2) an award or benefit that motivates a person to act

innovative new, inventive, or original

inspire to stir emotion, drive, or intellect as a means to motivate

integrity (1) pride, honor, and sincerity; (2) honesty, sincerity, and morality

L

law of supply and demand economic rule that states that businesses exist to supply goods and services that the consumer demands

leadership dynamic the pattern of changing systems and relationships that occur between leaders and the people they lead

leadership vision the ultimate goal or outcome a leader directs his or her team toward

liability area of potential legal responsibility

long-term goal an ultimate goal of any effort

M

majority more than half

manage to run, handle, or direct a system, task, or person

mediation a process where an outside party is brought into to help resolve a conflict

micro-manage to overmanage by frequently meddling, supervising, or making unneeded corrections

misconduct knowing and deliberate act of unethical or illegal behavior

motivate to encourage someone to act

motivation what drives us to act; the reason or drive to do something

multitasking working on more than one task at the same time

N

negligent indifferent, careless, or casual about duties

P

prioritize to order ideas, items, or tasks according to importance

production cost how much it costs companies to produce the goods and services they plan to sell

productivity amount of work completed per period of time

profit the money made by selling goods or services after production costs have been substracted

proposal an idea presented for approval

prototype nonworking model of a product

Q

quality control a specific strategy to ensure quality

R

reliable dependable; a person or thing that can be depended upon

responsibility an obligation or task for which you are accountable

responsible (1) to be reliable and trustworthy and concerned for your responsibilities; (2) to be accountable or answerable for actions, jobs, people, or things

S

short-term goal an attainable objective that helps achieve a greater goal

status quo commonly accepted belief or standard practice

T

take initiative act of your own accord

tendency an impulse to act a certain way

tolerance respect of the beliefs and practices of others

U

unanimous in complete agreement

W

work ethic the sense of duty that you bring to your work